Literacy in the Secondary School

Edited by Maureen Lewis
and David Wray

David Fulton Publishers
London

David Fulton Publishers Ltd
Ormond House, 26–27 Boswell Street, London WC1N 3JD

First published in Great Britain by David Fulton Publishers 2000

Note: The rights of Maureen Lewis and David Wray to be identified as the editors of this work has been asserted by them in accordance with the Copyright, Designs and Patents Act 1988.

Copyright © Maureen Lewis and David Wray 2000

British Library Cataloguing in Publication Data
A catalogue record for this book is available from the British Library

ISBN 1–85346–655–7

Typeset by Kate Williams, Abergavenny
Printed in Great Britain by The Cromwell Press Ltd, Trowbridge, Wilts.

Contents

Contributors

Maggie Croxford is Inspector for English in the London Borough of Greenwich, and a link inspector for 3 large secondary schools. She has had extensive experience of managing Borough wide literacy projects over the last 5 years. She currently manages the Greenwich literacy team and leads on the implementation of the National Literacy Strategy and several other major literacy projects within the Borough. She has worked closely with Val McGregor, the SRB secondary literacy co-ordinator on literacy across the curriculum at key stages 3, 4 and 5. Before taking up her present post in 1990, Maggie was a senior teacher for staff development and Head of English in one of the Borough's secondary schools.

Douglas Greig is head of Geography at Thomas Tallis Secondary School in the London Borough of Greenwich, where he also teaches history and religious education. He is a graduate of the University of Cambridge and has worked at the school for five years, since completing his PGCE at the Institute of Education in London. His main interests are in the development of resources to enhance literacy skills within the humanities curriculum, the management of literacy development at the level of the classroom and the school, and how student's learning can become more effective across the curriculum. He has delivered a number of INSET courses on these topics to practising teachers in and around Greater London.

Barbara Hersey, who has a Dip. Ed in Special Needs in addition to her degree qualifications is the Special Educational Needs Coordinator (SENCO) at South Dartmoor Community College in Asburton, Devon. The school is a mixed comprehensive with 1,200 students. Barbara leads a team of highly professional Learning Support Assistants and together they focuses on raising literacy achievement across the curriculum; on promoting strategies to aid this process and at increasing staff awareness of the issues involved. Barbara also has responsibility for the college's 'Re-tracking Initiative', which is aimed at preventing the exclusion of students whose behaviour can often be closely linked with literacy difficulties. She promotes close liaison with the college's feeder primary schools to enable her to be involved with students at an early stage and ensure literacy continuity.

Bob Jones is Head of Geography at Alleynes School, Stone.

Karen Kitt is Head of English at Plumstead Manor Comprehensive School in south-east London

Maureen Lewis is a Senior Lecturer in Language and Literacy at the University of Plymouth and is well known for her work as co-director of the influential Nuffield EXEL Project. She was a teacher in London for many years before beginning her research career at the University of Exeter, where she worked on several literacy research projects. She has written many books, chapters and articles about literacy including books on writing frames and the award-winning *Extending Literacy: children reading and writing non-fiction*, co-authored with David Wray. She has spent the last two years working closely with secondary schools as they address the challenges of supporting literacy across the curriculum.

Penny Manford is currently employed as Literacy Consultant for the Birmingham KS3 Literacy Project. As a mainstream secondary special needs teacher in nine different schools within the West Midlands, she has taught a variety of subjects. The roles of SENCO and Co-ordinator of Learning Development afforded her the opportunity to develop her interests in how pupils learn, and to explore cross-curricular strategies for the development of literacy skills. She has a keen interest in research and has undertaken many action research projects into aspects of literacy. Her current research, as an EdD student with the Open University, is an ethnographic study of the changing literacy practices which pupils encounter as they move from primary to secondary school.

Val McGregor is Secondary Literacy Co-ordinator for the London Borough of Greenwich. Prior to this, she worked in Inner London for ten years, an English teacher, followed by four years as an advisory teacher. She has also worked for the Open University as Staff Tutor for the London and Cambridge regions, contributing to the development of their P.G.C.E. course. In addition she has worked closely with Goldsmiths' College P.G.C.E department and, most recently, has contributed to their cross-curricular programme, and their distance learning materials for returners to the teaching profession.

Diane Swift is a former adviser for geography and assessment with Staffordshire LEA.

Penny Travers taught French and English and worked as a support and advisory teacher before taking up her current post of Ethnic Minority Achievement Adviser. She is committed to inclusive approaches and works alongside teachers in multilingual classrooms. Partnership teaching, she believes, offers a way of maximising the strengths of colleagues and is a powerful model of collaboration for pupils. She is particularly interested in development work and in scaffolding the curriculum to support and challenge pupils and unleash creativity. She has recently carried out action research in conjunction with the University of Cambridge School of Education on the impact that the learning environment and teachers' thinking can have on pupil progress.

Dennis Vickers teaches geography at Alleynes School, Stone, and has a particular interest in students with special educational needs.

David Wray taught in primary schools and is currently Professor of Literacy Education at the University of Warwick. He has published over 25 books on aspects of literacy teaching and is best known for his work, with Maureen Lewis, on the Nuffield Extending Literacy (EXEL) Project, which has been concerned with helping learners of all ages access the curriculum more effectively through literacy. The work of this project was made an integral part of the National Literacy Strategy and David was a founding member of the Advisory Group to the National Literacy Project. His major recent publications include: *Extending Literacy, English 7-11, Developing Children's Non-Fiction Writing* and *Writing Frames*.

Acknowledgements

We would like to thank first all of the schools in Greenwich, Enfield, Swindon, Devon and Birmingham whose teachers have contributed in no small way to the project from which this book stems. A book such as this is very much a collaborative enterprise and we are indebted to the teachers who have worked with us, not just for allowing us into their schools and classrooms, but for the quality of the ideas they have given us. We would also like to thank the following schools for the figurative materials in Chapter 3: Hatcham Wood, Lewisham; Lea Valley, Enfield; St Paul's R.C. School, Greenwich; Kidbrooke School, Greenwich: and St Thomas' School, Exeter and Chace School, Enfield for the illustrative material in Chapter 11.

We would also like to offer our very deepest thanks to the Nuffield Foundation, in particular to Helen Quigley, for having faith in us (and for providing the funding). We hope that the EXEL project may be considered to have been a successful use of that funding.

Introduction

Literacy is on the agenda in a big way in the United Kingdom. A reforming government with education as its highest priority has enabled developments on a scale we have rarely witnessed, and the initiatives are not complete yet. The principal target of the National Literacy Strategy from 1997 till the middle of 1999 was the practice of teaching literacy in primary classrooms. From 1999, however, the target has broadened and now clearly encompasses secondary school teaching as well.

Such attention, the history and context of which we catalogue in Chapter 1 of this book, has its positive and its negative sides. On the positive side, it is cheering to see the problems in literacy which many youngsters still have on moving to the secondary school at last given the attention they need. It is also a positive move to consider deliberately the role which subject teachers of all disciplines can have in enhancing the literacy achievements of their pupils. A literacy which is no longer seen as the sole responsibility of the English or Special Needs department has a much greater chance of flourishing and developing to meet all the requirements the twenty-first century will make of it.

On the negative side, however, we need to acknowledge the very real and practical problems such a focus on literacy causes secondary schools and, particularly, secondary teachers. Very few secondary teachers, even of English, have received any substantial training in literacy work and, if they are to respond in the best way possible to current initiatives, they need help – help of a very practical nature which enables them to introduce more effective attention to literacy into their subject teaching.

It is as an initial source of such help that this book is conceived. It stems from our work on the Nuffield Extending Literacy (EXEL) Project, during the course of which we have worked closely with secondary teachers in a number of cities, boroughs and counties, to assist them to develop the place and nature of literacy within their subject teaching. We have worked with teachers of Mathematics, Science, History, Geography, English, Technology and Modern Foreign Languages, and in inner-city, suburban and rural secondary schools. In the course of this work we have amassed dozens of teaching ideas and a fair sense of what works and does not work in terms of enhancing secondary school literacy. We aim in this book, with the help of several teachers, advisers and consultants who have worked with us, to provide an account of the good practice we have encountered and we hope that, at this early stage of the literacy initiative, this may offer some valuable practical support to secondary schools and teachers.

The book is structured into three basic sections. In Chapters 1 to 4 we cover a great deal of the background to our work, providing an overview of the current literacy initiative, an account of the frameworks of thinking underpinning the work of the Nuffield EXEL project and of how these translate into classroom action, and a description of one attempt to build from these frameworks a responsive method of assessing pupil progress in literacy across the curriculum.

Chapters 5 to 8 then take us very firmly into the classroom. These provide a series of accounts of classroom practice written by the teachers responsible for this, and covering areas such as Geography, English and Science. There are lots of practical examples here of how teachers have taken ideas and made them their own, and along the way produced some excellent teaching of literacy through the medium of their different subjects.

The penultimate chapter focuses on the wider, but still practical issues of what the school or local education authority can do to enhance literacy work at secondary level and we conclude with some advice about the devising and implementation of a secondary school policy for literacy.

The book then has as its audience all those with an interest in developing literacy at secondary school level, from teachers of all secondary subjects, to school literacy consultants and managers, to local education authority literacy personnel. We hope it will prove useful.

Maureen Lewis and David Wray
October 1999

Chapter 1

The current context – a brief history

Maureen Lewis and David Wray

There is always a great deal of interest, from the teaching profession, the general public, government agencies, the world of work and from the media in issues concerning literacy. Often such interest is expressed as a series of 'crises' or 'battles' such as 'falling standards', 'boys failing to read' or 'real books versus phonics'.

That such issues are perennial does not, however, mean they are irrelevant. Once again we are in the midst of a renewed interest and focus on literacy and it is instructive to review the context in which the current Key Stage 3 initiatives (to promote increased attention to literacy teaching within our secondary schools) occur. Much has happened in the area of literacy in the secondary school within the last two or three years and the rapid pace of change continues – prompted in part by the DfEE nationwide secondary literacy conferences held in the Summer term of 1999. These have made every secondary school in England aware that literacy is 'on the agenda' for they have set schools the challenge of drawing up, implementing and monitoring literacy action plans.

The current interest in the development of literacy throughout the secondary school must also be placed in the longer time frame of a curriculum cycle that began with the report *A Language for Life* (commonly known as the Bullock Report) published nearly 25 years ago (DES 1975). We must also consider the evidence concerning literacy achievements within our schools. This chapter will consider these matters in order to give a context and overview to the work that is to be described in subsequent chapters.

Literacy standards

Comparing standards of literacy over time is notoriously difficult. There are problems concerning what is being compared, whether compatible measurements are being applied and whether comparable groups are being compared. Despite these difficulties, comparisons continue to be made. Many people, however, accept that comparing statistical evidence of declining standards over time can be a 'red herring'. What the most recent statistics do seem to show is that, whatever the historical comparisons might be, in both national and international reviews of current evidence, standards of literacy in the United Kingdom are not high enough for a sizeable proportion of our students (Brooks *et al.* 1996). Such evidence suggests that such students are likely to struggle to cope with the literacy demands of a complex technological society.

There are a variety of sources of evidence that literacy remains a problem for many adults in England today. The most recent report on adult literacy (DfEE 1999a) claims that an estimated 'seven million adults in England cannot locate the page reference for plumbers in Yellow Pages'. Statistics produced by Ekinsmyth and Bynner (1994), ALBSU (1995) and UNESCO (1999) broadly agree that between one sixth and one eight of adults in Britain have literacy problems. Of the 12 OECD nations surveyed in 1997 for low levels of adult literacy and numeracy, only Poland and Ireland emerged with a lower level than Britain (DfEE 1999a).

With school age children, current evidence from the national testing of pupils in English at 11 and 14 years indicate that 30–40 per cent of pupils fail to achieve the reading standards expected for their age group. In the writing tests an even larger proportion do not attain the average score for their group (see Table 1.1).

	1997	1998
11 year olds at Level 4 or above	63%	65%
14 year olds at Level 5 or above	56%	

Table 1.1 Pupils achieving the average or above for their age group in the standard assessment tests for English

To this statistical evidence we can add the comments of Her Majesty's Inspectorate recorded in their *Review of Secondary Education 1993–97* (DfEE 1998a). HMI found that nationwide:

> standards of reading are good in six out of ten schools (*but*) they remain unsatisfactory in around one in seven.

HMI specifically identified that 'many pupils have weak skills in using non-fiction' and that:

> departments fail to provide tasks which challenge pupils as readers or offer reading experiences which enrich and extend the subject beyond the confines of the text book. Furthermore pupils are not taught how to make effective use of information from books, or the CD-ROM.

With regard to writing the report comments that:

> Standards of writing, however, were judged to be weaker, with about one fifth of secondary schools having pupils whose standards in writing were 'poor or very poor'.

There seems therefore to be evidence from a variety of sources that secondary schools do need to give greater consideration to supporting the literacy development of their pupils. Pupils leaving Key Stage 2 with an English SAT assessment of Level 3 (Level 4 being the expected norm) seem to be a particular focus for concern for the present government. Such pupils are unlikely to be 'statemented' but will nevertheless struggle with the literacy demands of the secondary curriculum. Initiatives such as the Summer Literacy Schools for Year 6 pupils about to join secondary schools are targeted particularly at 'Level 3' pupils and this and other current initiatives will be discussed later in the chapter.

New government – new priorities

Even while it was still in Opposition the Labour Party signalled that it regarded the raising of standards in literacy as one of its educational priorities, publishing an interim report on the thinking of its Literacy Task Force – *A Reading Revolution: How we can teach every child to read well* (Literacy Task Force 1997). In this report it indicated its belief that the, then pilot, National Literacy Project provided a model of literacy teaching for primary aged children that could be implemented more widely. Following the Labour Party's election to government in May of 1997 this interim report was followed by the final report of the Task Force, *The Implementation of the National Literacy Strategy* (DfEE 1997a). This document was sent to schools but it is doubtful that it found an audience amongst many secondary teachers as much of the report was devoted to literacy in the primary years. The final section (paras 108–120) did however deal with literacy in secondary schools and set out a clear statement of principle:

> Every secondary school should specialise in literacy and set targets for improvement in English. Similarly, every teacher should contribute to promoting it . . . In shaping their plans it is essential that secondary schools do not see work on reading and writing as exclusively the province of a few teachers in the English and learning support departments. (para. 112)

The report also made specific recommendations relating to secondary schools, all of which were to be implemented to one degree or another over the following year. These included recommendations that:

- there should be an HMI study to find evidence of where and how comprehensive, deliberate and intensive approaches work (para. 114);
- there should be a GEST (now renamed 'Standards Fund') funded development programme to help secondary schools to improve literacy (para. 115);
- the TTA should make a unit on the teaching of reading and writing a requirement of secondary teacher training and should develop criteria for such courses (para. 117);
- when the National Curriculum is revised the Curriculum Authority 'should consider the case for ensuring that: explicit and systematic attention to the skills of reading and writing becomes a feature of the programmes of study in relevant subjects' (para. 118);
- this Authority should also consider whether secondary schools should be able to concentrate intensively on literacy in Year 7;
- in their strategy for literacy, local education authorities should give attention to creating and maintaining cooperation between secondary schools and their feeder primary schools (paras 119–120).

The outcomes and implications of these recommendations

The HMI survey

During the Autumn term of 1997, HMI visited 49 secondary schools identified by LEA advisers/inspectors or HMI as schools involved in local, regional or national literacy development interventions as well as to those having a more general focus on language across the curriculum. These visits sought to identify 'what active measures successful secondary schools take to improve literacy standards, for all pupils but particularly for those whose literacy levels on entry are low' (para. 1, DfEE 1997b).

The report began by defining literacy and, significantly, went beyond a simple functional definition of literacy by identifying the importance of oracy and new forms of literacy such as on screen literacy. Its definition of literacy included the importance of literacy to the world of school, to life within wider society and in the personal growth of the individual. 'It enables pupils to gain access to the subjects studied in school: to read for information and pleasure; and to communicate effectively. Poor levels of literacy impact negatively on what pupils can do and how they see themselves'(para. 3, DfEE 1997b). Like the Task Force report quoted above, this report also stressed the role of teachers other than English teachers in supporting literacy.

The report drew seven key conclusions.

(i) Secondary schools are at a comparatively early stage in the development of pupils' literacy but successful practice is already evident in some.

(ii) There is no 'quick-fix' solution for deficiencies in literacy.

(iii) Considerable efforts are often put into literacy development but many schools do not monitor or evaluate the outcomes of their efforts.

(iv) A multi-strategy approach to literacy development is more likely to be successful than the adoption of a single strategy.

(v) Approaches that involve curriculum areas other than English, together with work done in English departments, are more likely to be successful than initiatives that are confined to English and/or SEN departments.

(vi) There are other 'literacies' besides reading and writing which schools need to develop, for example pupils' information literacy.

(vii) Literacy development is inextricably connected with the development of the whole young person and is linked to pupils' perception of themselves and their place in the world.

Many of these early conclusions were reinforced by further HMI reports (Robinson and Hertrich 1998) on the pilot KS3/4 literacy projects begun in September 1998 (see below) and were incorporated into the conference materials disseminated at the Summer 1999, Literacy Conference (DfEE 1999b).

Pilot Secondary Literacy Projects 1998–9

In September 1998, 22 local education authorities (LEAs) began Key Stage 3 literacy initiatives financed by the DfEE Standards Fund. Sixty-three bids had been submitted from the over 100 LEAs. In selecting successful bids the DfEE (DfEE 1998b) concentrated on those 'bids which focused on literacy development in Year 7 and the crossover from primary to secondary'. In doing so the DfEE could be seen to be signalling that it wished secondary schools to be aware of, and building upon, the changes to literacy teaching that were underway in primary schools as part of the National Literacy Strategy. It also looked for:

- well planned and coherent intervention programmes designed to raise literacy standards at Key Stage 3;
- the involvement of heads, governors and senior staff in the management of literacy in schools;
- whole school involvement – literacy development across the curriculum;
- community and library service involvement;
- language development models designed to raise boys' literacy achievement;
- paired reading and pupil tutoring schemes;
- programmes for tackling literacy issues for those for whom English is an additional language;
- effective evaluation strategies.

The criteria for successful bids can be seen to include a mixture of management objectives, teaching and learning objectives, targeting of specific groups of pupils as well as *all* pupils, monitoring and assessment objectives and the trialling of some specific teaching strategies. The importance of management issues as well as the use of curriculum strategies in establishing successful practice is well recognised and the key factors which need to be considered in implementing effective literacy policies are discussed in Chapter 11.

Link HMIs were assigned to each project and an interim report on the projects was published by HMI after one term (Robinson and Hertrich 1998). In this interim report ten critical dimensions arising from the projects were identified and in a further report John Hertrich (1999b) identified 18 issues arising from HMI inspections of the projects. These issues 'provide an agenda' that HMI feel all secondary schools might wish to address as they begin to implement literacy initiatives. They include considering:

- What is meant by a literate secondary age pupil?
- What strategies and structures are necessary to sustain literary development beyond Year 7?
- Is literacy development for all? What are the particular needs of boys, EAL pupils and higher attainers?
- What is the relationship of literacy development to English and to existing SEN work?
- What kind of guidance do schools need?
- To what extent can/does literacy development entail a 'dumbing down' of English?
- What level of knowledge about language do teachers need?

Hertrich elaborates on each of these issues (and the other 11 identified) by drawing on the evidence of best practice identified in the HMI visits. The HMI reports on the projects provide a useful overview of problems and challenges that face schools, as well as indicating some examples of good practice. The reports of individual projects written up by LEA personnel and teachers contain many interesting and innovative ideas. Unfortunately there is no central source to which interested readers can go to obtain any project outcomes and so these can best be obtained by using the contact details given in Appendix 1 at the end of this chapter which lists the authorities involved and the focus of their initiatives.

Many of the 22 successful authorities had already begun authority-funded initiatives prior to the 'Standards' funding and many have also continued to put local authority funding or alternative funding into the initiatives after the end of the one year of government funding. The government funding for the initiatives was only for one school year (1998–9). The very short term nature of this governmental 'pump priming' funding seems at odds with the recognition that 'secondary schools are at a comparatively early stage in the development of pupils' literacy and there is no "quick-fix" solution for deficiencies in literacy' (DfEE 1997b). The whole issue of funding for literacy development in schools is one that does not yet appear to have been addressed other than for those 900 secondary schools who hosted Summer Literacy Schools in August 1999 (see p. 11). These schools received £11,000 each to run the Summer school and implement a literacy programme into Year 7 during 1999 to 2000. The remaining schools (approximately a further 2,600 in England) have received no additional funding.

Literacy training for secondary teachers

As yet little has been done, since the publication of *The Implementation of the National Literacy Strategy* report (DfEE 1997a), to address the issue of training potential secondary teachers to be aware of the literacy demands of their subject. There is anecdotal evidence that several teacher training institutions are adding 'literacy' courses to their secondary programmes but this is not yet a statutory requirement. However, given the demand that all teachers should be teachers of literacy it seems self-evident that subject specialist teachers, both located within teacher training courses and those already in school will need advice on how to proceed.

As part of our Nuffield funded 'Accessing the Curriculum Through Literacy' project we undertook a survey of secondary teachers' views on literacy in 1998. The questionnaire data (Lewis and Wray 1999) shows that three quarters of the teachers surveyed had received little, or no mention of, literacy teaching during their initial teacher training courses (31.7 per cent of the sample had had one lecture, 44.3 per cent had had no training at all). Respondents overwhelmingly felt that literacy work should be a compulsory part of secondary teacher training (87.5 per cent) and so it seems reasonable to suppose that the government's recommendation on this matter will be widely welcomed by the profession. Only four per cent of respondents thought there should not be any literacy element in their training. Many teachers also felt moved to raise the issue of their own current training needs concerning literacy, in the comments sections of the survey. A typical comment was:

> *Massive* INSET needs to go on, to reinforce, and to establish good practice across the whole teaching staff.

How such training should be delivered to teachers already in schools is problematic. The national, school-based literacy training that is an integral part of the implementation of the National Literacy Strategy in primary schools was the first time such a programme had been undertaken. It is too early yet to judge its impact but OFSTED's interim evaluation of the primary NLS claims that effective implementation of the training provided for schools 'invariably produced a positive impact on staff attitudes and on motivation and on the quality of teaching' (OFSTED 1999, para. 64). No such package is currently envisaged for secondary schools and it appears that although LEAs and other INSET providers may offer training for secondary schools the take up will depend upon the individual vagaries of school budgets and priorities.

It is not just subject specialists who would welcome literacy training. There is evidence that even many secondary English teachers feel unsure how best to proceed in supporting literacy development. In a recent survey of all KS3 teachers of English in Northern Ireland, Collins and Dallat (1998) report that:

> One of the most striking findings of the survey is that many English teachers believe they do not have the necessary training or skills to meet the needs of the weak and failing readers in their classes.

and they quote comments such as:

> I have taught English for over twenty years and attended teacher training college before that. I do not consider myself trained to teach secondary level pupils to read. (p. 468)

Evidence of need is apparent and the issue of training concerning literacy development for both existing and trainee teachers is one that must be addressed.

Revising the National Curriculum

The role of literacy in subject areas has been considered in the recent review of the National Curriculum (QCA 1999). In this, a new statutory requirement is proposed which has been developed to be more explicit about how subject teachers should contribute to pupils' ability to use language in different curriculum contexts. The review proposal states:

> Pupils should be taught in all subjects to express themselves correctly and appropriately and to read accurately and with understanding. Since standard English, spoken and written, is the predominant language in which knowledge and skills are taught and learned, pupils should be taught to recognise and use standard English.
>
> • In writing, they should be taught to use correct spelling and punctuation and follow grammatical conventions. They should be taught to organise their writing in logical and coherent forms.
> • In speaking, pupils should be taught to use language precisely and cogently.
> • Pupils should be taught to listen to others and respond and build on their ideas and views constructively.

- In reading, pupils should be taught strategies to help them read with understanding, locate and use information, follow a process or argument and summarise, synthesise and adapt what they learn from their reading.

Pupils should be taught the technical and specialist vocabulary of subjects and how to use and spell these words. They should also be taught to use the patterns of language vital to understanding and expression in different subjects. These include the construction of sentences, paragraphs and texts which are often used in a subject, e.g. language to express causality, chronology, logic, exploration, hypothesis, comparison and how to ask questions and develop argument. (QCA 1999)

In order to support secondary schools as they implement this new statutory requirement QCA subject officers are currently preparing guidance and exemplars showing progression from Year 7 to Year 9 in the use of language in individual subjects in the secondary curriculum. These materials will be ready during 2000. They will build on and develop the series of leaflets published by SCAA in 1997 – *Use of Language: A common approach* (SCAA 1997). These documents gave useful examples of best practice. As Elizabeth Plackett has pointed out, they contain restatements of some of the ideas first raised in the Bullock Report (1975), 'albeit framed in a less generous and humane way' (Plackett 1999). Useful though these documents are, their impact appears to have been limited. In our many visits to secondary schools and conversations with secondary teachers over the last two years, we have found that few teachers seemed to know of their existence, or had them filed away and had made little real use of them. With the strong emphasis on literacy now evident at state, LEA and school level, coupled with the proposed statutory nature of the language statement quoted above, the new leaflets may prove to have a more ready audience.

Concentrating on literacy at Year 7/liaison with primary schools

There are several interrelated issues to consider when looking at what has happened and is likely to happen regarding the *The Implementation of the National Literacy Strategy* report's recommendation that, in relation to literacy, attention should be given 'to creating and maintaining cooperation between secondary schools and their feeder primary schools' (paras 119–120, DfEE 1997a). These issues include:

- the transfer and use of information regarding literacy levels of individual pupils as they move from primary to secondary school;
- curriculum progression from primary to secondary schools;
- the introduction of a literacy hour and framework of literacy teaching objectives for Year 7;

- the introduction of Summer Literacy Schools;
- Year 7 intervention programmes.

Liaison with primary schools – information transfer and curriculum progression
Many secondary schools pride themselves on their pastoral links with their feeder primary schools and have well-developed prior visiting and induction programmes in place for Year 7 pupils. However, recent research has shown that curriculum focused liaison presents a 'much more varied picture' (Schagen and Kerr 1999, p. 86). This research found that few Year 7 teachers were aware of what and how children had learnt in the primary school and that whilst 'secondary teachers were aware that the National Curriculum had brought changes to teaching and learning approaches, particularly at the top end of the primary school . . . They had little idea of what those changes were.' The introduction of the literacy hour has made this situation even more acute.

This research also found that the use of Key Stage 2 data to facilitate progression, in order that a pupils could start work at an appropriate point, was 'limited' and that many secondary schools adopted a 'clean slate approach' – starting pupils at a point they deemed appropriate and ignoring evidence of prior learning. Thus, this recent research confirms evidence from other research and reports which draw similar conclusions (Huggins and Knight 1997, QCA 1998, Goringe and Mason 1995, Lee *et al.* 1995). It would seem that the problems for secondary schools centre around:

- when and in what form secondary schools receive information from primary schools;
- whether secondary staff have a clear understanding of what the information tells them (for example, what does Level 3 in English mean?);
- how much trust they place in the validity of the information;
- whether systems are in place for them to see for themselves what is happening in literacy teaching and learning in primary schools.

LEAs and schools are aware of these problems and many of the pilot projects mentioned above included visits to primary schools for secondary teachers so they could see the teaching methods and strategies used in the literacy hour. Cross phase moderation and observation are powerful ways of helping teachers understand what happens at different phases of our school system. Many authorities are also looking at how to improve the transfer of data. For example, Bristol LEA is looking at transferring KS2 data via an Intranet to speed up the process.

Teachers' concerns about the validity of the KS2 data are well documented (Brookes and Goodwyn 1998, Schagen and Kerr 1999), and it is perhaps not surprising that this should be so as research confirms that many children do indeed experience a dip in achievement over the summer months. In an overview of 39 research studies (see Cooper *et al.* 1996, quoted in Sainsbury *et al.* 1998) such a dip was noted in most cases. The attainment of middle class pupils did not decline as much as other pupils but all the studies indicated that scores fall or do not move up over the summer. Similarly Galton found that about 40 per cent of pupils do less well in first year of secondary than they did in last year of primary school (Galton 1987). However, it would seem that the reasons for such a dip rests not on validity of the tests (these are usually well validated tests) but rather, Sainsbury (1998) speculates, upon several factors. These include:

- a lessening of the curriculum emphasis in the final term of Year 6;
- high motivation factors being in place for the May tests;
- pupils' anxieties about changing schools;
- the negative factors involved in being tested on entry;
- and the impact of the summer holiday itself.

Whatever the reasons for the dip, its practical outcome is that secondary teachers mistrust KS2 test results and many secondary schools administer their own tests to pupils on entry. Whilst it is not within the scope of this chapter to offer solutions to this problem, Schagen and Kerr make the point that greater understanding of what primary children can do in Year 6 may help reduce the need for re-testing and the 'clean slate' curriculum.

Summer Literacy Schools / Year 7 intervention programmes

One attempt to overcome the 'dip' and also offer literacy booster classes has been the provision of Summer Literacy Schools, in 1998 and again in 1999. Nine hundred schools took part in 1999 and integrated with these Summer schools was an expectation that the host secondary schools would carry the work on, into a Year 7 intervention programme. The guidance framework for these classes/Year 7 programmes stressed the importance of 'effective liaison with partner primary schools' (DfEE 1999c) and was considerably more prescriptive in the model it proposed than for the previous year. For those schools taking part the DfEE proposed:

- whole school management by literacy task group;
- close contact with primary schools;
- a Summer Literacy School which included at least 50 hours of dedicated teaching of literacy;
- bridging activities to boost pupils' reading and writing skill, including booster groups at Year 7, vacation packs for pupils unable to attend classes and literacy based linking projects between Years 6 and 7;
- a reception programme for pupils joining the secondary school to include parents' meetings, reading mentors, personal targets and the use of literacy diaries;

- a coordinated literacy curriculum at Year 7 including planning to objectives from the NLS framework and tightly structured lessons based on the NLS model;
- an integrated assessment programme.

Whilst acknowledging that this represented a 'challenging programme', the guidance notes claimed it was 'necessary if schools are to address systematically the needs of pupils transferring to secondary schools with significant deficiencies in their skills as readers and writers'. It is too early yet to assess whether those schools taking part have been managing to meet these challenges but the model and the Year 7 draft framework also promoted via the guidance document appear to be spreading beyond the original 900 schools.

The literacy hour and framework of teaching objectives
The suggested Year 7 framework, which is based on objectives taken from the primary framework, is reproduced at the end of this chapter as Appendix 2. Those schools taking part in the 1999 Summer schools were encouraged to implement this framework. Several of the LEA pilot projects (for example, Nottingham, Bristol and Islington) have also tried aspects of the framework and the introduction of a literacy hour. Introducing a literacy hour often raises the issue of where the time is to be found within the crowded secondary timetable. Some schools have located it within the English timetable; others have taken time equally from English, humanities and maths/science to create literacy hour slots, and others still, have encouraged departments apart from English to include a literacy hour approach within their teaching. Video material, showing a history teacher conducting a history lesson via the literacy hour structure of whole class, group work and a plenary session whilst paying attention to both literacy and history teaching objectives, was sent to every secondary school as part of the conference materials (DfEE 1999a). While not insisting that every secondary school should adopt a literacy hour and/or the framework, there appears to be a strong steer that schools should at least consider adopting such an approach. Given the emphasis on certain teaching methods and the need for considerable English subject knowledge embedded within implementing an effective literacy hour, adoption of a literacy hour at Year 7 would seem to raise again the issue of training and support for secondary teachers.

Looking back to the Bullock Report

The brief history we have offered of the initiatives over the last two years gives some sense of the huge impetus that is building up around improving literacy at Key Stages 3 and 4. We have made no mention yet of the myriad other initiatives that have been taking place in authorities and schools not included in the pilot projects such as those in Greenwich (see Chapter 10) or Lewisham. Nor have we mentioned the research and curriculum development work being undertaken in collaboration between universities, LEA personnel and schools such as our EXEL project (Wray and Lewis 1997), Christine Counsell's work for the History Association (Counsel 1997), Eve Bearne's work with secondary schools (Bearne 1999) and Webster *et al.*'s work with Bristol schools (1996). Nor have we mentioned other significant indicators of growing interest such as the launch of a new magazine for secondary English teachers and the many courses being offered linking literacy and curriculum subjects as KS3 and 4. The cumulative effect of all these events is a sense that the 'literacy initiatives' are once more firmly on the educational agenda.

For those teachers over 45 however, their interest in new developments may be tempered with a slight feeling of *déjà vu* for they will recall the Bullock Report (*A Language for Life*, DES 1975) and its effect. This report argued that all teachers were teachers of language and for a few years after its publication it had a great impact in secondary schools, prompting a review of curriculum materials, the setting up of many school working parties and the creation of Language across the Curriculum policy documents. This work was given further impetus by the outcomes of important research projects such as *The Effective Use of Reading* (Lunzer and Gardner 1979).

That the Bullock Report had a great impact at the time but that this failed to last is widely acknowledged, and different reasons have been put forward for this. Bearne (1999) ascribes it to institutional problems in that paper initiatives never became embedded in school practice. Brookes and Goodwyn (1998) suggest that 'the movement was gradually subsumed by the reform of the examination systems, the introduction of TVEI and other "reforms". To this must be added the introduction of the National Curriculum and its impact in focusing teachers' attention upon the content and pedagogy of their discrete curriculum areas.

We will examine in more detail in Chapter 11 the issues that can help ensure that literacy initiatives have a lasting impact but it is also worth noting the shift in emphasis that has taken place since the publication of the Bullock Report. Bullock stated that:

> In the secondary school all subject teachers need to be aware of:
>
> (i) the linguistic processes by which their pupils acquire information and understanding, and the implications for the teacher's own use of language;
> (ii) the reading demands of their own subjects, and ways in which the pupils can be helped to meet them.
>
> To bring about this understanding every secondary school should develop a policy for language across the curriculum. The responsibility for this policy should be embodied in the organisational structure of the school. (DES 1975)

It is notable that there is an emphasis on oral language and its role in developing understanding (and hence, by implication, learning). However, there is no mention of writing and the emphasis appears to be on creating a policy rather than on practical actions. In contrast, the statement of principle in the 'Implementation of the National Literacy Strategy' document makes no mention of oral language but does include writing.

> Every secondary school should specialise in literacy and set targets for improvement in English. Similarly, every teacher should contribute to promoting it ... In shaping their plans it is essential that secondary schools do not see work on reading and writing as exclusively the province of a few teachers in the English and learning support departments. (para. 112)

In the latest statement of principle (the QCA draft proposal, see p. 8), all three elements (oral language, reading and writing) are acknowledged and QCA gives a clear steer to practical manifestations of its overall demand by mentioning specific forms of reading and writing and uses of oral language. While some elements of the QCA statement may cause dispute (the insistence on standard English, and the specific references to subject teachers teaching punctuation and spelling, for example), it seems to us significant, that after 25 years, we at last have a statement that includes all aspects of language and literacy development and one that recognises that often action must precede written policy documents.

Given the events of the last two years and the impact of the literacy conferences for all secondary schools held in the summer term 1999, the next few years are going to be important in supporting the role of secondary teachers in developing language and literacy through their subjects. In the next two chapters we shall consider why and how they might do so by focusing upon the model of teaching effective interactions with non-fiction texts that has resulted from the work of the Nuffield EXEL Project and upon the practical applications of this model.

Chapter 2

Extending literacy: learning and teaching

David Wray and Maureen Lewis

Introduction

For a number of years we have been involved in a project funded by the Nuffield Foundation which has been exploring ways of helping teachers to extend their pupils' literacy. The main focus of the Nuffield Extending Literacy (EXEL) Project has been to devise and trial in classrooms a range of strategies whereby teachers might develop the abilities of their pupils to use literacy more effectively as a means of learning. Our work has, therefore, tended to concentrate upon the reading and writing of non-fiction text, an area which has been rather neglected in the past in terms of both research and the development of practice. This is also, of course, an area in which the concerns of primary and secondary teachers overlap. Literacy is the key to learning in all areas of the curriculum at all ages.

Central to our work has been our attempt to establish a theoretical basis for teaching pupils how to learn with texts. This theoretical base has two aspects. Firstly, we have developed a model which describes the processes involved in this learning with texts. This we have christened the Extending Interactions with Texts, or EXIT, model. It has come to have substantial influence upon the work of primary teachers, largely through being used to underpin the 'Reading and Writing for Information' module of the National Literacy Strategy training materials, studied by staff in every primary school in England during 1998–9.

The second aspect of our theoretical base is our conceptualisation of the effective teaching of literacy for learning as a four-phase process. This builds upon a great deal of earlier and well known work on teaching and learning processes and dovetails strongly with the teaching processes implicit within the National Literacy Strategy. Perhaps most importantly, it readily provides a practical set of teaching strategies to implement the important theoretical ideas of modelling and scaffolding.

The accounts of school and classroom developments which make up the bulk of the present book have all been influenced to a degree by both these sets of ideas and it will be useful at this point in the book for us to outline some of the thinking and research underlying them.

Learning with texts

The processes involved in using literacy to learn have tended to be described in the literature as 'information skills' and, in that they refer to the processes of locating and dealing with the information given in texts in a range of media, this is a useful descriptor. We are concerned, however, that the use of this term, and linked terms such as 'information reading' and 'study reading', tends to indicate a separation of these ways of interacting with texts from ways more generally referred to as 'reading'. As Cairney (1990) has argued, theories about the understanding of written text which characterise it as a process of information transfer, that is as 'getting the information from the text', are strongly contradicted by more recent conceptualisations of the reading process as one of transaction, that is, the active construction of meaning in negotiation with the text as written (see Rumelhart 1985, Goodman 1985). Thus any model aiming to describe the process of interacting with expository texts must account for its transactional nature and build in a strong element of the reader contributing to the constructed meaning.

Almost all the attempts which have so far been made to elaborate more fully what happens when we read and learn from expository texts have tended to term themselves as descriptions of the 'information process'. Winkworth (1977), for example, suggested an analysis consisting of six stages of activity:

1. Defining the subject and the purpose of the enquiry.
2. Locating information.
3. Selecting information.
4. Organising information.
5. Evaluating information.
6. Communicating the results.

These six stages were used by Wray (1985, 1988) to form a basis for advice to teachers on the teaching of information skills through class project work. Models such as this are useful as guides for teachers to the processes through which their pupils might go as they pursue project enquiries. They suffer, however, from the major problem that they are incomplete. They lack what we now feel to be the crucial element of the actual interaction with a text. In the terms of these models, what happens when a reader faces the words on the page of an appropriate text is limited to selecting, extracting and recording information. This now seems inadequate as a description of the multifaceted transaction between a reader, coming to a text with a whole range of attitudes, feelings and arrays of knowledge, and the words on a page, created by an author with a range of intentions, many of which go beyond the simple passing on of information.

The EXIT model

In presenting a model which we hope represents a more complete description of the processes involved in learning with texts, we are immediately faced with the difficulty of representing a complex and essentially recursive set of processes in the two-dimensional space defined by print on paper. Although, in what follows, the model will be represented as a series of numerical stages, it is important to realise that this is for convenience only. We do not intend the model to be read as a linear description of what happens when we interact with information texts.

We see the process of learning from, with and through texts as involving ten kinds of mental activities, as follows.

1. Elicitation of previous knowledge.
2. Establishing purposes.
3. Locating information.
4. Adopting an appropriate strategy.
5. Interacting with text.
6. Monitoring understanding.
7. Making a record.
8. Evaluating information.
9. Assisting memory.
10. Communicating information.

We shall give a brief description of and rationale for each of the ten 'stages'. In the following chapter we will describe and illustrate some appropriate teaching strategies linked to this model.

1. Elicitation of previous knowledge

It has become quite clear from learning theory that, in order for any real learning to take place, we have to draw upon knowledge we already have about a subject. The more we know about the subject, the more likely it is that we shall learn any given piece of knowledge. Learning which does not make connections with our prior knowledge is learning at the level of rote only, and is soon forgotten once deliberate attempts to remember it have stopped. (Most people can remember times they learnt material in this way, usually as preparation for some kind of test: once the test was over, the information 'went out of their heads'.)

Learning has been defined as 'the expansion and modification of existing ways of conceiving the world in the light of alternative ways' (Wray and Medwell 1991, p. 9). Such a constructivist approach to learning places great emphasis upon the ways in which prior knowledge is structured in the learner's mind and in which it is activated during learning. Theories about this, generally known as schema theories as they hypothesise that knowledge is stored in our minds in patterned ways (schema) (Rumelhart 1980), suggest that learning depends, firstly, upon the requisite prior knowledge being in the mind of the learner and, secondly, upon it being brought to the forefront of the learner's mind. Any model, therefore, which attempts to act as a guide for teachers to develop their pupils' abilities to learn from texts, must include an emphasis upon the need to elicit what the learners already know about the topics of these texts.

2. Establishing purposes

A crucial part of the process of learning from texts must involve the specification of what information is required from these texts and why. If this is not done, then subsequent interactions with texts will tend to be haphazard rather than purposeful. For many pupils, however, an initial purpose for reading will often consist of nothing more than a vague statement such as 'I want to find out about dinosaurs (or birds, or trains, etc.)', which is certainly not precise enough to be useful to them. Statements like this have two logical consequences. Firstly they give no criteria for judging the usefulness of any information which is found. If it is about dinosaurs (or birds, etc.) then it must be relevant. Secondly there is no indication of when the process of finding information should stop. Pupils could go on for ever finding information about dinosaurs (etc.) and still be no nearer satisfying this vague purpose.

They need instead to be encouraged to specify as precisely as possible what it is they want to find out, and what they will do with that information when they have found it. They may be asked to draw up a list of questions to which they want to find answers, or tasks which they aim to complete. Such question-setting is itself not unproblematic, but its key function of making work with non-fiction texts more purposeful is of undeniable importance. We should bear in mind, however, that question-setting may not always occur at the beginning of a project. The EXIT model is not intended to be seen as linear in its operation and it is quite likely that question-generation will occur and reoccur as the project progresses.

3. Locating information

Clearly, in the world outside school, the texts which will help meet the reading purposes pupils have defined will not be simply presented to them as a package. They will need to find the information they require in libraries, books or whatever sources are appropriate. This will involve knowing how to use a library system to track down likely sources of the information required, how to find information efficiently in books and other sources (using index and contents pages, for example), but also how to use the most important information resource – other people. To this list must also be added the skills of using the various tools of information technology to retrieve needed information. Teletext televisions, computer databases and the Internet are all extremely useful sources of information in the classroom, but not unless the pupils possess the requisite skills for using them. These location skills are not actually terribly complicated, yet pupils and adults alike often seem to have difficulties in using them. From our own research (Wray and Lewis 1992) it seems common for pupils to be able to explain perfectly well how to use an index to a book, for example, but then, when left to their own devices, to prefer to leaf through a book instead. There appears to be a problem of transfer of learning here as the pupils we studied had certainly been taught about locating information in books and libraries. They had just not transferred this knowledge into action. We would suggest that the solution to this problem is to make sure that pupils are taught to locate information within the context of actually doing it, usually as part of an investigative project. If this is done, pupils will be much more likely to use browsing as a deliberate strategy in book use rather than as their only strategy.

4. Adopting an appropriate strategy

It is clear that efficient readers modify the ways they read according to their purposes for reading, the nature of the texts they are faced with and the context in which they interact with these texts. Compare, for example, the different ways the following reading tasks would usually be approached:

(i) Finding a telephone number in the Yellow Pages.
(ii) Reading a newspaper over the breakfast table.
(iii) Studying a textbook chapter in preparation for a test.

In the first example, the reading would involve glancing over several pages of text looking for a particular word or group of words. When this was found, a closer reading of the particular item of information would follow. This reading strategy we generally refer to as 'scanning'.

In the second example, the major part of the reading would involve the rapid browsing through large portions of text, gaining a fairly general picture of what the items and articles were about. Some of these items would probably receive more detailed attention than others, but most would not be read in close detail. This approach to reading is usually termed 'skimming'.

The third example is very different in that it would probably involve the close reading, and perhaps re-reading several times, of every word in the chapter. Such 'intensive reading' is comparatively rare in non-educational settings, but where it is appropriate, it is usually very important that it is done effectively.

   From research into the capacity of readers of various kinds to monitor and control their own reading behaviour (Wray 1994) it appears that one of the things which distinguishes effective from less effective readers is the ability to take appropriate, and conscious, decisions about which reading strategy to adopt in which circumstances, and when to switch strategies. Pupils need to be shown how to read different kinds of materials in different ways and also how to make decisions for themselves about the appropriate strategies to use in particular situations. We suggest that an important teaching strategy towards this is for the teacher to demonstrate appropriate ways of behaving, that is for the teacher to model how he or she reads a particular information source, thinking aloud as he or she does it so that pupils can gain an understanding of how and why reading strategies are selected.

5. Interacting with text

The above processes are crucial to the effective use of reading to learn and, in many ways, the success of the actual 'eyeball-to-text' part of the process depends upon them. Nevertheless, it is the stage of interacting with the text which remains at the heart of the whole process. Here the reader engages in an intricate transaction with the printed symbols, constructing a meaning, or meanings, on the basis of what he or she brings to the text – knowledge, beliefs, attitudes – and the intended message of the author of that text. In order to help pupils engage in this process more successfully, we suggest that teachers might employ strategies which focus pupils' attention on the ways in which texts are constructed and the ways in which meaning is created and might be recreated. Activities such as cloze procedure, sequencing and text restructuring, given the generic title of DARTs (Directed Activities Related to Texts), have been quite extensively researched (Lunzer and Gardner 1984, Wray 1981) and appear to be useful in enabling this interaction with text. Other strategies, such as text marking (by underlining, highlighting or numbering), have not been so widely researched but our classroom work suggests they have some success in helping pupils focus on the sections of texts most relevant to their reading purposes.

6. Monitoring understanding

Current theories of reading tend to converge in suggesting that an important element of the comprehension process is the reader's ability to monitor his or her own understanding as it develops in interaction with a text, and to take remedial action in the event of comprehension problems. Reading for meaning therefore involves the metacognitive activity of comprehension monitoring (Brown 1980). Although mature readers typically engage in comprehension monitoring as they read for meaning, it is usually not a conscious experience. Skilled readers tend to proceed on automatic pilot until a triggering event alerts them to a failure or problem in their comprehension. When alerted in this way they slow down and devote extra effort in mental processing to the area which is causing the problem. They employ debugging devices and strategies, all of which demand extra time and mental effort.

Realising that one has failed to understand is only part of comprehension monitoring; one must also know what to do when such failures occur. This involves the making of a number of strategic decisions. The first of these is simply to decide whether or not remedial action is required. This seems to depend largely upon the reader's purposes for reading (Alessi *et al.* 1979). For example, if a reader's purpose is to locate a specific piece of information, a lack of understanding of the surrounding text will not usually trigger any remedial action. On the other hand, if the purpose is to understand a detailed argument, then practically any uncertainty will spark off extra mental activity.

In the event of a decision to take action, there are a number of options available. The reader may simply store the confusion in memory as an unanswered question (Anderson 1980) in the hope that the author will subsequently provide sufficient clarification to enable its resolution, or the reader may decide to take action immediately, which may involve re-reading, jumping ahead in the text, consulting a dictionary or knowledgeable person, or a number of other strategies (Baker and Brown 1984).

Numerous research studies have examined pupils' monitoring of their own comprehension and it is possible to draw some fairly firm conclusions. According to Garner (1987), 'The convergent findings from recent research can be summarised: Young children and poor readers are not nearly as adept as older children/adults and good readers, respectively, in engaging in planful activities either to make cognitive progress or to monitor it. Younger, less proficient learners are not nearly as "resourceful" in completing a variety of reading and studying tasks important in academic settings' (p. 59).

It seems that one important area upon which the teaching of reading to learn needs to focus is pupils' awareness of their own understanding as they read. As with the adoption of an appropriate reading strategy, we suggest that the most effective teaching strategy for this is for teachers actively to demonstrate to pupils their own thinking/monitoring processes as they try to understand a text. It has been demonstrated that the systematic use of such thinking-aloud can have significant effects upon pupils' abilities to understand what they read (Palincsar and Brown 1984).

7. *Making a record*

In adult everyday life, a search for required information will not always result in any written record: the adult may simply remember the information or act upon it immediately. However, in the effective use of reading as a means of study, in schools or colleges, the recording of information, usually by the making of notes, will be an essential part. Yet it appears that even for students in higher education, who have presumably developed effective ways of studying, instruction in strategies for recording information is minimal or non-existent (Wray 1985).

In our attempts to develop effective teaching strategies in this area we have been strongly guided by two principles. One of these concerns the need to consider information recording as inextricably linked to the purpose for reading. It would make little sense to teach pupils to take notes as they consult information sources without giving consideration to why they will need these notes and to why they are looking for this information in the first place. To neglect the link between purpose and recording is to risk leaving pupils in the position of feeling that they have to note down all the information they read which is in the least bit relevant. Sometimes, of course, this will seem to be all the information and note-making then descends to the level of copying.

The second principle which has guided us has been that, although skilful adult note-makers might well develop their own note structures to fit particular purposes and texts, younger students will need their initial attempts at note-making quite heavily scaffolded by structures suggested by their teachers. We have been experimenting here with a range of grids and frames to provide this scaffolding and have found some evidence that pupils can begin to make their own decisions about note-making as they see for themselves the usefulness of guiding structures.

8. *Evaluating information*

In the light of the 'information explosion' we are currently witnessing, with the sheer amount of textually stored information growing exponentially far beyond an individual's capacity even to be aware of its existence, it seems even more important that we try to develop in pupils a questioning attitude to what they read. Many adults retain an inherent propensity to believe that 'if it says it in print, it must be true', yet most would accept that it would not be good for pupils to be taught to believe everything they read. A useful definition of literacy claims that it involves 'having mastery over the processes by means of which culturally significant information is coded' (de Castell and Luke 1986: p. 88). If this is accepted, it implies that the literate person, far from being controlled by the manifestations of literacy, should, in fact, be in control of them. This involves having some autonomy in the process of using literacy, and having the ability to make choices. Propaganda and publicity rely for their effect upon recipients' lack of autonomy, and their sometimes overpowering influence upon the choices made.

Developing the abilities, and willingness, of pupils to be critical of what they read will involve encouraging them to use a variety of criteria to judge the accuracy, relevance, and status of the information they find. They will naturally tend to believe that everything they read in books written by adults who know a great deal more than them about a particular topic is bound to be true. Yet they will constantly come across examples of misleading and biased information, and they need to know how to recognise this and what to do about it.

We suggest that one teaching strategy to develop this questioning attitude is for the teacher deliberately to confront pupils with examples of out of date, biased or contradictory written material and to encourage them to discuss these features explicitly. Obvious possibilities for this include dated books, different newspaper reports on the same events and advertising material. In leading this discussion the teacher can provide a model of how he or she goes about evaluating what is read.

9. Assisting memory

Although more recent psychological research into memory has suggested that this is a good deal more complex than we might at first think, one very influential way of examining memory has been to look closely at its corollary, forgetting. Experiments have revealed that we tend to forget the majority of the facts we try to learn by heart within about 24 hours. Our rate of forgetting then slows down considerably and we may maintain our memory of the residue for a much longer period (Ebbinghaus 1966). Such insights do not provide much cause for confidence that pupils' location of information in texts will have much long-term impact upon their knowledge, a somewhat depressing suggestion for heavily content-based curriculum areas. Other research has, however, made it clear that there are factors which can influence memory and forgetting and which can positively inform teaching strategies (Child 1973).

Firstly, it seems that the more meaningful the information we are trying to remember, the more likely we are to retain it for a longer period. Meaningful information is information which the learner can make sense of, that is, can 'fit' somewhere in a mental map of that part of the cognitive world. This re-emphasises the importance of attempting to bring to the foreground learners' previous knowledge which, as we suggested earlier, is the key to effective learning.

Secondly, remembering is improved by revisiting the information one is trying to remember. This is well known by secondary teachers who often explicitly ask their pupils to 'revise' material. Often, however, this revision may be too far removed from the initial learning and can turn into an almost complete re-learning. In our work with teachers we have suggested strongly that pupils need to be given plenty of opportunities to work with information if they are to remember much of it for longer than a few days. This may involve restructuring information into different formats, re-presenting it to other people and using it in different contexts.

10. *Communicating information*

In many adult information-using experiences, telling other people what has been found is not an important part of the process simply because the outcome may well be some kind of personal action rather than a report of whatever kind. Yet in educational contexts physical outcomes, usually written, are almost invariably expected of pupils as part of their work with information texts. As we have just argued, this can be a benefit in helping pupils make the information they are working with more their own, and thus retained for longer. Yet there is some concern that pupils are often fairly limited in the kind of written outcomes they produce as a result of work with information.

For one group of theorists (e.g. Martin 1985, Christie 1985) this problem is defined as one of genres, by which they mean particular textual structures fitting particular communicative purposes. They argue that the vast majority of pupils' non-fiction writing is actually a form of recount, that is, they simply tell the story of what they have done and found out about a topic. There are a range of other written genres, far more common and useful in adult life, such as reports, discussion papers, arguments, which pupils are hardly ever encouraged, or taught, to produce.

If this line of argument has any merit, then teachers need to give more attention to enabling their pupils to communicate what they have discovered and learnt through work with texts in a wider range of textual forms. We have been working quite intensively on the idea of using framework written structures to help pupils experience a range of ways of presenting information and ideas. These seem to act as a form of scaffolding for pupils' non-fiction writing and we have some evidence that pupils begin to take the structures and use them spontaneously for their own purposes.

Teaching the effective use of texts

Developing effective teaching of any subject would be impossible without a thorough understanding of learning. Children's learning is the intended outcome of all teaching and, while it would not be true to say that we currently know everything there is to know about learning, we have amassed over the past decades a great deal of soundly based knowledge about learning and the learning process. This knowledge has come partly from scientific research, often conducted in laboratories and under clinical conditions (the work of Piaget is one example of this) but also validated and extended by work in real classrooms (much of Bruner's work, for example). It has also been enriched by theoretical developments which have changed the ways we commonly think about learning (Vygotsky's insights are perhaps the best example of this). From current insights into processes of learning it is possible to describe some principles which underpin effective teaching of literacy.

Principles for teaching

There are four major principles for teaching which emerge from insights into learning. These have relevance across the curriculum but are particularly important when considering the teaching of literacy and language.

Principle 1
Teachers need to ensure that learners have sufficient previous knowledge and/or understanding to enable them to learn the new things planned for them. They also need to help learners make explicit the links between what they already know and what they are currently learning.

Principle 2
Teachers need to make provision for group interaction and discussion as part of their teaching, giving pupils opportunities to engage in guided work both in small, teacherless groups and in groups working alongside experts. For group interaction to truly take place, and to be beneficial in learning, the activities planned for pupils need to demand more than that they simply sit together: they have to be planned so that discussion is an essential part of them.

Principle 3
Teachers need to ensure meaningful and appropriate contexts for learning, particularly in basic literacy skills. Children need to be taught the skills they need in settings that are as close as possible to those in which those skills are regularly used. Decontextualised exercises, for example, are not likely to be effective as a long-term teaching strategy.

Principle 4
Teachers should try to promote learners' knowledge and awareness of their own thinking and learning. This might be done by, for example, encouraging them to think aloud as they perform particular cognitive tasks. It will also be achieved through the essential teaching strategy of teacher demonstration.

Towards a model for teaching

Palincsar and Brown (1984) describe a teaching procedure that begins from the principles just outlined. Working with the aim of improving students' abilities to respond effectively to text, they begin by arguing that most attempts to train students to do this have produced rather discouraging outcomes. Teaching has apparently had little real impact upon learners' use of strategies for making sense of textual materials and, particularly, on the transfer of these strategies to activities outside those directly experienced during the teaching context. This failure to effect real change in learners' approaches to dealing with text they attribute to a model of learning which sees learners as simply responding, relatively passively, to instruction without really being made aware of just what they are learning and why. They claim that teaching, to be successful, needs to encourage learners to be active in their use of strategies and to understand why, and when, they should use the strategies to which they have been introduced.

The model of teaching they propose as an alternative arises from the ideas of Vygotsky (1962/1978), who put forward the notion that pupils first experience a _particular cognitive activity in collaboration with expert practitioners. The learner is firstly a spectator as the expert (parent or teacher) does the majority of the cognitive work. The learner then becomes a novice as he or she starts to take over some of the work under the close supervision of the expert. As the learner grows in experience and capability of performing the task, the expert passes over greater and greater responsibility but still acts as a guide, assisting the learner at problematic points. Eventually, the learner assumes full responsibility for the task with the expert present still in the role of a supportive audience.

Using this approach to teaching, pupils learn about the task at their own pace, joining in only at a level at which they are capable – or perhaps a little beyond this level so that the task continually provides sufficient challenge to be interesting. The approach is often referred to as an apprenticeship approach.

The distance between the level at which pupils can manage independently and at which they can manage with the aid of an expert is termed by Vygotsky 'the zone of proximal development'. This, according to the model of teaching that has begun to emerge from these ideas, is the area in which the most profitable instruction can proceed. Vygotsky claimed that 'what pupils can do with the assistance of others might be in some sense even more indicative of their mental development than what they can do alone' (1978 p. 85). What they can do collaboratively today becomes what they can do independently tomorrow.

There appear to be four stages to the teaching process implied by this approach.

(i) Demonstration

During this stage, the expert models the skilful behaviour being taught by demonstrating it in action. Thus a teacher might read to a group of pupils from an enlarged text which they can all see clearly. An important function of this shared reading is to provide a model for the pupils of how such a text can be read. The teacher therefore ensures he or she shows such features of reading as:

• predicting what might be coming next;
• reading and interpreting diagrams and pictures;
• using book features such as an index in an information book, etc.

There is some evidence that learning can be assisted if this modelling is accompanied by a commentary from the expert during which his or her thinking about the activities being undertaken is made explicit. One relatively simple procedure is that of the teacher modelling how he or she tackles the skills being taught, that is, reading or writing in such a way that the learners have access to the thought processes which accompany these activities. Tonjes (1988) discusses metacognitive modelling as a way of teachers demonstrating to pupils the reading and comprehension monitoring strategies which they use and argues that teachers using this approach should concentrate upon modelling mental processes – what they think as they read or write – rather than simply procedures – what they do. Only in this way, she suggests, can pupils learn strategies that they can apply across a range of situations rather than which are limited to the context in which they were encountered.

(ii) Joint activity

The expert and the learner share the activity. This may begin by the expert retaining responsibility for the difficult parts while the learner takes on the easy parts, while in some teaching strategies prior agreement is reached that participants will take turns at carrying out sections of the activity. The expert is always on hand to take full control if necessary. One of the best examples of this joint activity is that known as 'paired reading' (Morgan 1986) in which the teacher (or parent) and the learner read aloud in unison until the learner signals that he or she is ready to go it alone. The teacher withdraws from the reading but is ready to rejoin if the learner shows signs of difficulty such as prolonged pausing or reading errors.

(iii) Supported activity

The learner undertakes the activity alone, but under the watchful eye of the expert who is always ready to step in if necessary. This can be the stage in the process that is most often neglected and it has been suggested (Wray and Lewis 1997) that teachers tend to move too rapidly from heavily supporting pupils' work to asking them to work without support. Consequently, it is at this stage that there appears to be most need of practical teaching strategies.

(iv) Individual activity

The learner assumes sole responsibility for the activity. Some learners will, of course, move much more rapidly to this stage than others and the teacher needs to be sensitive to this. It is, arguably, equally as damaging to hold back learners by insisting they go through the same programme of support and practice as everyone else as it is to rush learners through such a programme when they need a more extensive programme of support.

Conclusion

The purpose of this chapter has been to outline the theoretical basis on which we have been trying to develop teaching strategies to help pupils respond more effectively to information texts. Although we have been at pains to stress the difficulties in devising models of this nature, we have found that the teachers with whom we have worked have reacted positively to this attempt to provide a framework for their classroom work.

Chapter 3

Theory into practice: strategies to support literacy development

Maureen Lewis and David Wray

In this chapter we will look at how the EXIT model, described in the preceding chapter, translates into actions and strategies in the classroom. We will outline generic strategies that can be used in a variety of curriculum subjects to activate prior knowledge, to introduce and use key words effectively, to develop interactive reading and to encourage purposeful note-taking. All subject departments can use these strategies, which are illustrated by examples from a range of departments and year groups. In the second section of the book (Chapters 5 to 8) teachers describe, through case studies, how such strategies can be integrated into units of work to support literacy development within their subject area.

Activating prior knowledge

Activating prior knowledge has an impact both on pupil learning and on supporting literacy. The strategies used to encourage pupils to think about what they already know about a subject and its links with their own lives inevitably engage them in using language to express ideas (however tentative). The vocabulary that arises from activities to activate prior knowledge may not be the technical language of a subject but will be related to key concepts and ideas around the topic. These can be developed in ways that enhances pupils' understanding of the topic, helps them recognise areas of enquiry and aids their understanding of key technical words. The main generic strategies for activating prior knowledge are:

- discussion;
- brainstorming / concept mapping;
- using visual sources;
- using artefacts;
- using grids, e.g. KWL grid.

Discussion

Traditionally, teachers have often begun a unit of work or a lesson by initiating a discussion which encourages pupils to think about what they already know about the subject. Discussion powerfully encourages shared thinking and verbalised learning (Slavin 1987). Discussion has several positive features: it is immediate; all pupils can participate, whatever their level of literacy; it can encourage pupils to articulate and recognise what they know; collaborative discussion can trigger new ideas; it creates opportunities to recognise, share and value different experiences and knowledge from a range of backgrounds and cultures, and key ideas and vocabulary can be introduced within a supportive context.

As well as class discussions, teachers can organise discussions in small groups with a report back session. Group organisation can encourage pupils who may be reluctant to participate in whole-class discussions and gives more pupils the opportunity to participate. Group discussion is often facilitated by having some ground rules which are explained to the class and reiterated frequently. These may be:

- everyone must participate;
- everyone must cooperate;
- everyone must know the answer, i.e. anyone in the group should be able to explain the group's thinking, and talk, acting as spokesperson.

Giving pupils a picture or artefact to prompt their discussion can provide a purposeful focus. At the report back session the teacher can scribe the responses, thus ensuring that key ideas are highlighted and the correct written form of key words are available.

However, most discussion is ephemeral – usually no record of what was said remains. The following strategies all provide written records of pupil thinking which gives teachers access to three important things:

- what pupils already know;
- what pupils do not know, i.e. the gaps in their knowledge;
- information about any misconceptions held.

Such information is important for planning purposes, for assessment purposes and for informing a record of what is know/unknown and misunderstood. It also offers the opportunity to make explicit to pupils that they have something to offer and an active part to play in the learning process. This may help increase their interest and motivation.

Brainstorming/concept mapping

Brainstorming is a simple, well-known technique whereby pupils, working collaboratively in pairs or small groups, discuss and note what they know about a topic. Figure 3.1 shows a brainstorm from some Year 8 boys thinking about what they know about the USA, at the start of a unit of work in geography.

Such brainstorms (sometimes called topic webs, word webs, etc.) can then be developed into concept mapping by encouraging the group to look at their initial brainstorm for words/ideas that are linked in some way. For example, the information in Figure 3.1 could be gathered together under headings such as sport, leisure, presidents, important monuments and so on. The drawing together of scattered ideas under concept headings often stimulates further ideas and yet more details can be added to the map. Deriving concept maps from initial brainstorms can also give teachers the chance to introduce more technical vocabulary. For example, the concept grouping 'monuments' may well be expressed in everyday pupil language as 'buildings'. Not only can the group's vocabulary be enhanced but they are also given contextualised access to the more technical vocabulary they will need to engage with during with the unit of work.

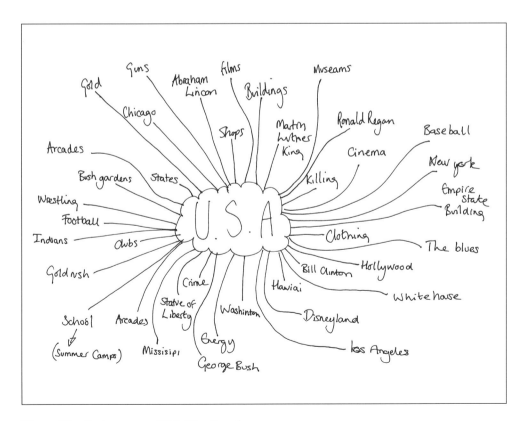

Figure 3.1　Brainstorm on USA. Year 8 students

Concept maps

Concept maps are another well-established way of activating prior knowledge. There are many different ways of undertaking concept mapping. The teacher may start the activity by providing a concept map with headings already in place and invite pupils to brainstorm around each heading. Figure 3.2 shows an example of a concept map for a Year 8 unit of work on energy.

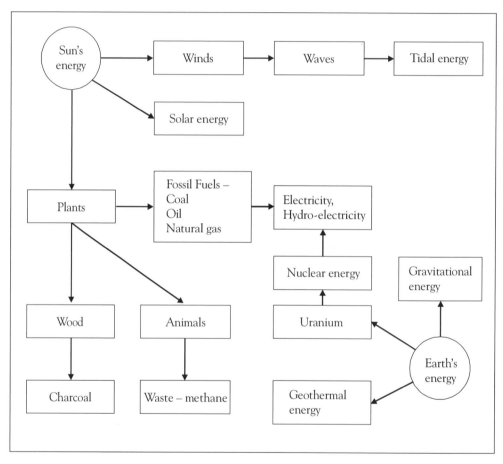

Figure 3.2　Starter concept map for pupils to add comments to linking lines, new linking lines and new idea boxes

Alternatively pupils can be given words or phrases, connected to the topic, scattered at random on a sheet of paper. Their task is to link any words which they see as having a connection. They write what the connection is upon the linking line. This strategy has the advantages of not only activating prior knowledge but also giving teachers evidence of misconceptions or partial knowledge. It can help pupils identify for themselves areas where they have gaps in their knowledge as they can place a question mark against any words they are unable to link in any way. They can also place a question mark against those items that they have tentatively connected but are unsure as to the accuracy of the link. After undertaking such an activity, pupils have a real purpose for undertaking reading about the topic, for they can confirm, add to or alter their maps in the light of subsequent reading.

Brainstorming and concept mapping can be used both before and after a unit of work, which will allow the maps to be compared. This usually, of course, will show the developments in the knowledge and understanding of a group of pupils, but it also allows for a rough and ready assessment of the group's progress. Individual concept maps can also be produced if more individual assessment is required. It can be useful to keep or display initial brainstorms and concept maps, encourage pupils to refer back to these and to discuss how their understandings have changed during the course of their work. Alternatively, initial brainstorms can be kept and new knowledge added (in a different colour pen) as it is acquired. This gives pupils an explicit record of their growing expertise in a particular area of knowledge. Pupils often take pleasure in such comparisons as it gives them concrete evidence of how their knowledge has increased in a particular subject.

Using visual sources and artefacts

Pupils can brainstorm around a picture or an artefact. Give pupils a picture, diagram, graph or artefact to examine and discuss. They write what they have learnt from it. If the picture has been taken from a textbook they can then be given the accompanying text and can check what in the text confirms what they have learnt from the visual source and what more information the text adds. Figure 3.3 shows a recording grid for this activity.

Pictures in books can be used by covering the text with paper or 'Post-it' notes leaving just the picture visible. Pupils list what they can see and what they think that tells them. In order to make these kinds of deductions they would have to draw upon their existing 'world' knowledge. They also make a list of any questions they want to ask as a result of their close study of the pictures. These pictures/lists are then passed on to another pair who repeat the process and add further observations/comments/ questions.

Another strategy is to show pupils the first few minutes of a video, then stop the tape, and then get them to discuss, and note, what they have learnt so far, anything it has made them think of, and what they think might be covered later in the tape. This strategy heightens pupils' metacognitive awareness by making them explicitly aware that learning is not a passive process. A learner is constantly making links between what they are seeing/reading/hearing and what they already know.

What I can learn from the picture

We learn that the wave has a lot of Energy. It needs it to turn over. The wave has a lot of Kinetic energy and not a lot of potential energy.

What I can learn from the text

The waves are caused by the wind it has a lot of Kinetic energy and we could use it to make energy for humans to use.

Wave energy

Waves are caused by the wind. They contain a lot of energy but it is hard to make use of it. One idea is to have floats that move up and down with the waves and so turn a generator.

What are the advantages of this type of energy?

The energy is renewable not man made.

What are the disadvantages?

The wave could be too strong and break the equipment.

Where does the energy come from?

The energy from the Sun makes the wind to move the sea.

Figure 3.3 Comments prompted by picture stimulus. Year 8 student

Using grids

There are many grids that can be used to record prior knowledge. One generic grid which has been extensively used is a KWL grid (Ogle 1986, 1989, Lewis *et al.* 1995). Each column of the grid (see Figure 3.4) refers to a different stage in the research process.

The advantage of this grid is that it both provides a written record and the format of the grid acts as a structural organiser, helping pupils see more clearly the stages of

What do **I know** about this topic?	What do **I want** to know about it?	What have **I learnt** about it?

Figure 3.4 KWL grid

their learning. The procedure is based on three cognitive steps – accessing prior knowledge, determining what needs to be learnt, recalling what has been learnt. The final column is filled in as a summary after the pupils have undertaken some research.

Key words

Key words can be either those specific to a particular subject (e.g. circulation, arteries) or words used across the curriculum that appear to present spelling challenges for a number of pupils (e.g. because, their/there). The latter category needs to be included in a whole-school spelling policy although many of the strategies listed below can also be used for 'whole-school' key words. Introducing key vocabulary within subject departments is well established as a strategy for supporting literacy in many secondary schools. In our survey of strategies used by subject teachers to support literacy, 89 per cent of the respondents claimed to use key words with their pupils (Lewis and Wray 1999). This wide usage may be because this strategy has both a subject-specific dimension as well as a literacy dimension. Focusing on subject-specific vocabulary is an obvious way in which literacy support can be contextualised and subject teachers can see benefits in that it enhances subject knowledge as well as helping with literacy. Introducing 'key words' may also offer an immediate and relatively simple way into addressing literacy support for teachers who have no training in literacy. This high usage of the introduction of key words does however beg the question of how this strategy is used and of its effectiveness. Our observations in schools show that often this does not go beyond identifying and displaying key words and some teachers need help in recognising how to use such words in more interactive ways with students.

Ten strategies for use with key words

The following strategies have proved useful.

1. Subject specific dictionaries

Several publishers are now producing inexpensive subject-specific dictionaries. These are useful in that pupils can more quickly locate words within these than in a large, general dictionary. The definitions also give the technical definition first rather than pupils having to seek it out amongst several everyday meanings. When a new key word arises, get a pupil to look up the word in the dictionary and read out the definitions. Discuss and clarify the meanings and get pupils to define the word in their own words. Encourage the use of these dictionaries on a regular basis.

2. Creating word banks

After brainstorming/concept mapping, key words from this activity are identified and written on strips of card by pupils. These are sorted and displayed alphabetically around the room. New key words are added at the end of each lesson, having first been identified and defined within the context of the lesson. Constantly revisiting the lists in this way reminds pupils of their extent and purpose. They should also have their attention drawn to the lists whenever they are undertaking written work. Pupils could also create their own word lists in the back of their workbooks or highlight the words in their subject dictionaries, if they have a personal copy.

3. Word and definition cards

In some schools, support staff have prepared boxes of cards for specific units of work. One set of cards contains the words, another definitions. These can be used for matching activities. If the separate words and definitions are placed on computer pupils can cut and paste their own prompt sheets.

4. Creating interactive glossaries

A list of key words from each unit of work (e.g. Year 10, Genetics and evolution) is drawn up and written into a folded A4 booklet, with the words listed alphabetically down the left hand side of the page and with a blank line alongside each word. This can be differentiated into separate booklets for pupils taking higher and lower GCSE papers as different vocabulary is required. A separate sheet of definitions is produced but these are jumbled up and do not match the order of the words in the booklet. Pupils are given a unit 'glossary', which contains the words but no definitions, to paste into the front of their workbooks. In each lesson two or three key words are stressed (some will be new words, some will be repeats from previous lessons) and used in context. In the last five minutes of the lesson the pupils find those key words in their glossary booklet. They then find the appropriate definition from the definitions sheet and use this to complete their own glossary by writing in the definitions next to the word. Thus key words are introduced in context and their meaning continuously revisited and revised (see Figure 3.5).

5. Key word crosswords/word-searches

Pupils complete crosswords based on key words and their definitions. Once created such crosswords can be stored on computer and become a permanent resource for the department. The crosswords can be of the conventional type with the key word definitions given as clues and the key words being filled in on the crossword grid. Alternatively pupils can be given a completed crossword grid and are asked to create the clues for each word. Each activity helps reinforce meaning as well as spelling.

Glossary Definitions: Genetics and Evolution

a gene that does not always show itself	a male or female sex cell
what we look like	surroundings in which an organism lives
what genes carry	a fertilised female gamete
the changes by which organisms have devel[oped] organisms	
the remains or shape lived a long time ago	
the survival of organ conditions they live	
producing new kind organisms by breed useful characteristi	
producing young b parents	
a sudden change of an organism	
a group of organ can breed togeth	
a particular vers for eye colour,	[con]trol
the joining together of a male and female sex cell	conditions t[he]
passing on of characteristics from one generation to the next	groups of *genetically identical* living things
the part of a cell that controls what happens in a cell	chromosomes are made of this

Glossary for unit of work on genetics and evolution

allele	
artificial selection	
aseptic technique	
characteristic	
chromosome	
clones	
DNA	
dominant	a gene that always shows itself
environment	surroundings in which an organism lives

Figure 3.5   Interactive glossary and definitions sheet. Year 10 unit of work

6. Creating word clusters

Draw pupils' attention to the patterns to be found in words (e.g. equal, equalise, equate, equilateral, equality, equation, equidistant equilibrium and so on), pointing out their common root (equa/equi, from the Latin word meaning to make even) and how that helps with both spelling and meaning. Pupils can create word cluster posters and display them in subject rooms.

7. Creating mnemonics

Mnemonics are sentences created to help us remember how to spell words or a sequence of facts. The first letter of each word in the sentence is significant. The well-known examples are ones such as 'Richard of York gave battle in vain' (r,o,y,g,b,i,v – the colours of the rainbow) or 'Big elephants cannot always use small exits' (because). For homework, pupils can create a mnemonic to remind them how to spell a key word. The results are shared and one is selected by the class to become their mnemonic of choice; this is written up, displayed and its use encouraged. Adolescents can often come up with very amusing ideas for mnemonic sentences. School mnemonics used by all staff and pupils for commonly misspelt words can be adopted. For example: to remember how many Ss and how many Cs are needed in the word 'necessary', the whole school could adopt the sentence, 'It is *necessary* for a shirt to have one *collar* and two *sleeves*'.

8. Creating calligram posters

Calligrams are visual representations of a word that reflect its meaning. For example, the word 'test-tube' might be written with an exaggerated letter u which takes on the shape of a test tube, or 'glacier' might be written in jagged, 'ice letters'. Again, pupils can create such visual representations of key words and display them for all to share.

9. Using icons

Icons and symbols alongside key words can act as memory prompts and are particularly useful for pupils struggling with literacy. Standard icons can be adopted across the school and can be used on worksheets as well as on word lists and wall displays. For example, a drawing of a pencil can always accompany the instruction 'write', or the outline tool shapes often used as an aid to effective storage in design and technology departments can have the word written alongside them also.

10. Playing word games

The final few minutes of a lesson can profitably be given over to word games that use key vocabulary. There are many such games. For example:

- Key words can be written at random on an OHP and projected onto a wall; for example in maths words such as quadrilateral, rectangle, square. When the teacher reads out a definition, two opposing team members compete to be the first to identify and touch the correct word.

- Half a word can be written on the OHP and members of opposing teams volunteer to complete the word.
- The traditional game of 'hangman' can be played on an OHP.
- Everyday terms such as 'times' and 'share' are written by the teacher and volunteer team members add the 'posh' versions – 'multiply', 'divide', and so on.
- You provide the definitions and pupils write the words.

Games such as these require little in the way of preparation, can end a session on an upbeat note and help revisit and revise key words in an active and engaging way.

Interactive reading

Reading is an important part of the learning processes but reading is neither a simple nor a singular activity. There are many processes involved in reading and there are different ways of reading (such as skim reading, scanning and close reading) depending upon our purpose for reading. There is much evidence to suggest that opportunities for sustained reading are limited in secondary schools and much reading is located within a particular type of text – the textbook. Subject teachers therefore have a role to play in encouraging reading, widening the range of materials read, encouraging a range of reading behaviours and helping pupils understand the materials they read. Building opportunities for ten-minute reading sessions into lesson times; setting dedicated subject reading homework; ensuring a wide range of library type information books are available and used within subject classrooms; having an 'in the news' notice board with current newspaper and magazine articles, etc., about maths, science, geography and so on would go some way to tackling the first two challenges. Teacher modelling, and tasks to encourage different reading behaviours, can be introduced and a range of interactive reading strategies can be used to promote understanding.

Teacher modelling and metacognitive discussion

Teachers can model different ways of reading to students (whilst also offering subject content) by reading aloud to pupils in a variety of ways and from a variety of texts as well as textbooks. By reading aloud to pupils, whilst they follow in a book or on a OHT, teachers can demonstrate what it is you actually do – not by merely telling but by showing and accompanying the showing with a monologue on thought processes they (a fluent reader) employ. Thus they can model how they actively interrogate and respond to a text – 'I wonder what that means? . . . Well that surprises me . . . I knew that' – as well as demonstrating scanning or tackling difficult words and so on. This kind of metacognitive modelling (Tonjes 1988) – making explicit to students the thought processes of a reader – gives less skilled readers vital lessons. The impor-tance of teachers not simply telling students about the problem-solving, planning and strategic decision-making which characterise the reading process, but actually demonstrating these cannot be over emphasised. Modelling enables teachers to make explicit the thought processes which accompany involvement in literate activities; processes which, by their very nature, are invisible. Unless these processes are made explicit, struggling readers have little way of understanding what it is like to think like an accomplished reader until they actually become one: in other words, much of their learning is directed towards an end, of which they have no clear concept.

Understanding text

A major part of our work in the EXEL project has been aimed at helping children engage in a variety of ways with the information text they have to read in school. Several of the strategies we have used are commonly known as DARTs activities (Directed Activities Related to Texts) and they were promoted by Lunzer and Gardner (1979, 1984) and their colleagues in a series of Schools Council projects. To our surprise, our survey of secondary teachers' literacy practices (Lewis and Wray 1999) found that, although DARTs activities such as text marking, sequencing, and cloze procedure are widely supposed to be commonplace in secondary school practice, more than half of secondary teachers claimed to use them 'rarely' or 'never'. Given their impact at the time of their introduction, their dissemination in published materials and the continued emphasis on these techniques in teacher training and INSET courses, it is surprising to see how infrequently many secondary teachers use them. This may reflect the amount of time needed to prepare such materials, the time needed to use such materials effectively in class or a lack of familiarity of these strategies on the part of the respondents. It could also be a manifestation of a lack of understanding of the need to get students to interact directly with challenging materials. The following strategies are all ways of encouraging pupils to actively engage with a text and do something with it, which demonstrates their level of under-standing.

Cloze

Cloze is an activity in which certain words in a passage of text are deleted and the students are asked to complete the text. It is an activity best used in pairs or groups rather than as a solitary activity, for much of its value lies in the discussion of possibilities. Completing a cloze text relies upon the readers actively striving to make the text make sense. In the following example students would complete the text by drawing on a variety of knowledge.

Mount St Helens – an exploding mountain

Mount St Helens is a (–A–) in the Rocky Mountain chain of North America. The Rocky (–B–) are fold mountains and form part of the North American plate. To the west of the Rockies lies the Pacific plate and the collision zone between the two (–C–). The fold mountains were (–D–) as a result of sediments being uplifted from the ocean floor as the (–E–) and North American plates collided approximately (–F–) million years ago.

Knowledge sources used would include the following:

• Using understanding of stylistic features of writing: e.g. at space (–A–) you could repeat the word 'mountain' but would be unlikely to do so as it would mean using it four times in two sentences.
• Using the sense of the whole sentence, i.e. the context: at space (–B–) reading on to the end of the sentence would prompt the missing word.
• Drawing upon knowledge of language structures (syntactic knowledge): at point (–C–) the missing word must be a plural noun as signalled by the use of the article 'the' and the adjective 'two'.
• Using existing knowledge: this can be recently acquired, that is, learnt from what you have just read up to that point as at point (–E–) or, can be information that you simply know or don't know as there is no clue given in the text, as at point (–F–).

Having finished the passage pupils should be encouraged to re-read through the whole piece to check the sense of the whole thing. The pairs/groups should then share their choices with the class so alternatives can be aired.

Sequencing

In text sequencing, jumbled up text is given to pupils who have to re-order it into a coherent, logical or sequential text. In doing so they must read and re-read the text to confirm their choices. Like cloze, sequencing can easily be differentiated by careful selection of text and is best undertaken as a collaborative activity, which encourages active discussion of meaning. Pupils' reconstruction may not be quite the same as the original order and this can provide a useful discussion point as pupils justify their ordering of the text. It is often best to allow pupils to physically move the text around and try out possibilities.

Text-marking

In text-marking activities students are encouraged to highlight or underline information, or numbers, or write comments in the margin of a text as they read. It is a
strategy for focusing upon particular parts of a reading and in order to identify the
items to be marked pupils must pay close attention to the text. Figure 3.6 shows a part
of a text on energy which pupils have text-marked. Using different colours to
differentiate categories of information makes it easier to relocate that information at
a later date and also enables multiple marking to take place.

Text-marking – the main idea/summaries

Pupils can be asked to underline what they think is the sentence that tells you most
about the passage. This may vary depending upon one's purpose for reading the
passage. Different pupils may choose to underline different sentences and this can be
used as a discussion point when pupils share and justify their decisions. They can also
be asked to underline the sentence which sums up each paragraph. Putting these
sentences together should give them an outline summary of the whole text.

Text-marking – making notes in margin

Pupils can also be encouraged to write notes in the margins of texts they are studying.
They could list out information they have identified, write down any further
questions that have arisen in their minds, note where something is not clear to them
with a question mark and so on. These activities help pupils recognise that reading a
text is not a passive activity but involves actively engaging with text in a variety of
ways.

Text-marking – numbering text to show a sequence of events

Text can also be numbered to identify sequences of events. This is especially useful
where individual steps in a process are elaborated upon and so the sequence process
being described is separated by chunks of explanatory texts. Struggling readers can
lose the thread of the basic events. A text that has been marked sequentially in this
way can then be used to create a flow diagram of the process.

Text restructuring

The essence of this strategy is to encourage students to read information and then
show the information in some other way. In doing so they have to 'pass the information through their brain' – that is, work at understanding it. Restructuring thus gives
teachers access to students' levels of understanding and so can also be a useful assessment tool.

Instructions
READ the passage.
UNDERLINE ONCE each object that has or uses energy (the first is done for you).
UNDERLINE TWICE the types of energy it has, uses or gives out.
COPY and COMPLETE the table below in your book.

Object	Types of energy
Lamp	Electrical, light

In your book DRAW an energy transfer diagram for each object. Follow the examples below:

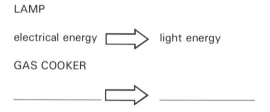

LAMP

electrical energy ⟹ light energy

GAS COOKER

David gets up at 7 o'clock on school days. He switches on a lamp by his bed. The lamp gives out light energy so that he can see. It uses electrical energy. He has breakfast in the kitchen. All the family eat eggs for breakfast. His mother cooks the eggs on her gas cooker. Gas has chemical energy. Eggs and other food also have chemical energy. This energy comes from the Sun. David will need the energy in food for all the things he wants to do.

A lamp uses electrical energy. It gives out light energy.

A toaster uses electrical energy. It gives out heat energy.

Jane gets up at 8 o'clock. She likes toast for breakfast. Her father makes toast with an electric toaster. This uses electrical energy. At half past eight she waits outside for David.

Jane and David go to school on a bus. The bus uses petrol. Petrol has chemical energy. It is made from oil. The engine changes the chemical energy into the movement energy of the bus.

Some chemical energy changes to heat energy. This keeps the bus warm in winter.

Figure 3.6   Text-marking – energy. Year 7 student

There are many different ways of text restructuring including:

- rewriting in a different style – for example, as a newspaper report or a science story;
- using grids;
- drawing annotated visual representations of what has been learnt (Figure 3.7);
- labelling diagrams (Figure 3.8);
- sorting text cards in different ways (Figure 3.9);
- pictograms, graphs and Venn diagrams.

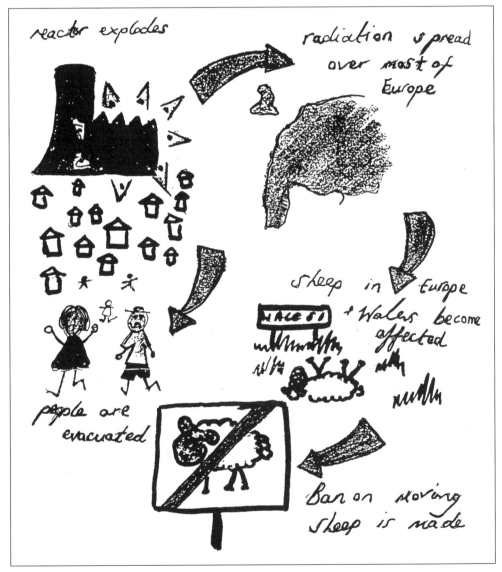

Figure 3.7 Annotated visual representations of the effects of the Chernobyl explosion. Year 9 student

Red blood cells have ___heamaglobin___ but white cells do not.

White cells have ___nucleus___ but red cells do not.

Blood flows through the organs of the body in capillaries.

PLASMA   Label parts of plasma.

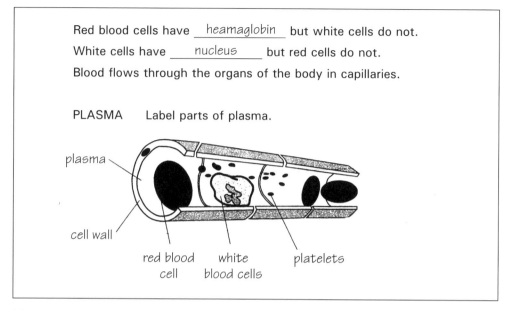

Figure 3.8   Labelling a diagram

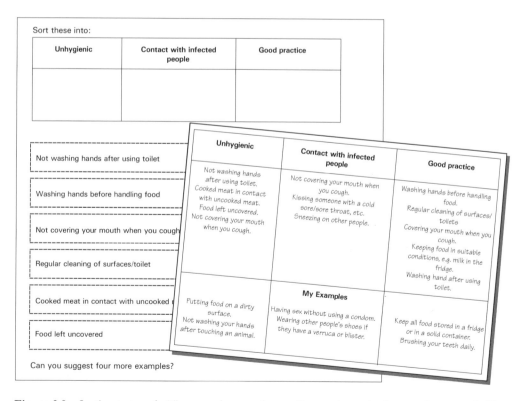

Figure 3.9   Sorting text cards. These can be sorted according to given criteria or students can decide on the criteria

This list is by no means exhaustive and most teachers will be able to add their own examples to those that we have provided. Teachers can suggest ways of restructuring the text read or can pose it as an open-ended task, i.e. 'Show me that information in another way'. The important principle however is to encourage pupils to engage in what Bereiter and Scardamalia (1987) would call a 'knowledge transforming strategy' rather than a mere 'knowledge retelling' strategy.

Note-taking

The ability to make notes from a variety of sources is an important skill in gathering information and one that is increasingly relied upon as pupils progress through the education system. It is still rare however, judged on our informal questioning of students of all ages, to discover many to whom note-taking has been actively taught. Most pupils appear to somehow 'pick it up' or 'work it out for themselves'. There are, however, many ways in which teachers can assist their students to become more efficient and effective note-takers.

As with any communication task it is important to know why we are undertaking the task and who it is for. There are several reasons why we might take notes and we should discuss the purpose of the notes with our pupils. It might include:

- helping scaffold their understanding of what is being read by
  - bringing about an active engagement with the text, e.g. underlining something because they think it is important
  - promoting concentration and focus by making notes as reading progresses;
- creating a record in preparation for doing something else, e.g. writing a report, making poster;
- creating a record for later use, e.g. for revisiting a few weeks later;
- acting as a brief *aide-mémoire* which will be discarded, e.g. as a prompt for a talk.

Pupils also need to understand that most notes are written for their own use, although they may occasionally share them with a group or partner. This means there is some freedom for them to invent their own abbreviations, visual prompts, and so on, as well as use standard abbreviations

There are several important note-taking procedures.

Finding key words/phrases
Use text highlighting, underlining or writing on a sheet alongside the text. Decide on those words which are crucial to the content.

Summarising

Find a key sentence to summarise each paragraph. (In study skills books this is often referred to as 'What's the main idea?'.) Put all the 'main idea' sentences together to create a précis.

Deleting

Leave out unimportant sentence creating words (e.g. 'and', 'the') as notes do not need to be in sentences. Leave out redundant material (e.g. repetition, unneeded details). Younger and less able pupils may need to cross out this redundant material, initially.

Substituting

Combine lists or groups of items when possible (e.g. 'apples, pears and grapes' could be written as 'fruit').

Abbreviating

Use standard abbreviations and signs (e.g. BBC, =, etc.). A good dictionary will have a list of them. Encourage students to create their own abbreviations (e.g. E1 for Elizabeth the First).

Recording sources

We need to record sources in case we ever need to return to them and in order that pupils begin to understand the niceties of acknowledging authors' works.

Teacher modelling of note-taking

The best way to introduce note-taking is via teacher modelling. Unless pupils experience what it is an expert note-taker does and what 'good' notes look like they are unlikely to have sufficient knowledge of the process to create their own notes. Modelling is more than getting pupils to passively copy teachers' pre-written notes from the board. Make notes from a source in front of the pupils whilst explicitly discussing what it is you are doing and why. Before beginning, the focus of the note-taking is made explicit: 'We're looking at Tudor food so I'm going to note down anything about food, cooking, meals, etc.' Talk about each of the procedures listed above as you use them and also demonstrate that:

- notes are not in 'best' handwriting;
- layout, writing size, asterisks, underlining, etc., can be used for emphasis rather than punctuation;
- headings and other forms of graphic organisers (see below) can help organise the notes;
- annotated drawings, visual prompts, rough graphs, etc., can be included.

Next use your notes to demonstrate their purpose. You could use them for oral recall or to create a piece of report writing. Gradually you hand over some of the process to the pupils in shared sessions before asking them to make notes in independent work. A useful intermediary stage can be for an adult to read the text aloud to pupils whilst they follow in their own copy of the text and then the adult re-reads the text as the pupils make notes. This can support the less fluent reader or support pupils in using more complex texts than they could manage independently. Display notes alongside any more elaborated finished outcomes so that the purposeful nature of note-taking is shown to be valued.

Some practical ways for supporting inexperienced note-takers are as follows:

Trash and treasure
Introduce the idea of 'trash' (words you do not need) and 'treasure' (vital words). Treasure words to be emphasised in some exciting way such as zigzag outlining.

Grids
Physically restricting the amount of space for recording reminds some pupils to use words rather than sentences. Grids with category heading already filled in help structure both the information finding and the recording process. Later, pupils can create their own grids. A generic note-taking grid is a QUADs grid (question, answer, details, source), see Figure 3.10.

Question	Answer	Details	Source

Figure 3.10   A QUADs grid (Cudd 1989, Wray and Lewis 1997)

Dividing the answer into two (answer and details, or colloquially, the short answer and the long answer) encourages pupils to record a brief summary first and then details as a series of points.

Diagrammatic representations (graphic organisers)
Spider diagrams (Figure 3.11) and tree diagrams (Figure 3.12) are different graphic ways of organising key ideas with lesser, but linked ideas coming from these. Structuring information in this way can then lead to using the structure for more extended writing. Provide pupils with the structure outline, initially, as this can help

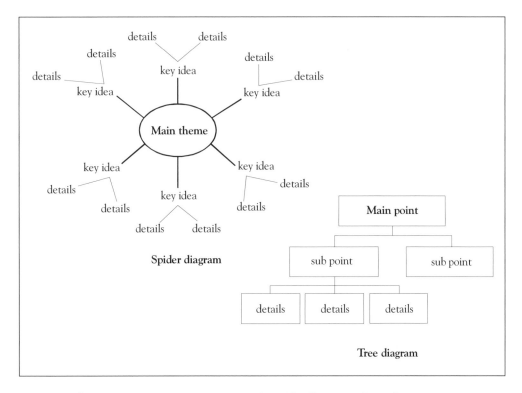

Figure 3.11/3.12   The organisational structure of a spider diagram and tree diagram

them by taking away some of the organisational demands, leaving them free to concentrate on content.

Christine Counsell (1997) suggests a similar organising strategy – sorting information into 'big points' and 'little points'.

Using headings
Lists and skeleton written outlines can be broken up with headings. Initially you may wish to supply the headings, plus a set number of empty bullet points to support pupils.

Playing the 'Notes Game'
Teachers can also refine pupils' note-taking skills by playing the 'Notes Game' in those few minutes before the end of a lesson. In this game the teacher writes a sentence about the current unit of work on the board and then asks, 'Who can give me this information in the fewest possible words?' Suggestions are written on the board until the minimum number of words needed to convey the information remain.

It can be useful to set note-taking as a homework task and comment constructively upon students' attempts, rather than regard notes as the unlooked at part of students' work.

Conclusion

The strategies described in this chapter all support both subject learning and literacy development. They encourage pupils to engage with the meaning of words and texts and demonstrate their understanding. Some activities encourage close reading of the text; others, such as text-marking, encourage scanning and skimming. It is important that, throughout, teachers take time to discuss with the students what it is they are doing – how they had read a particular piece, what decisions they made when undertaking some text restructuring, created notes and so on, for this all helps make the process explicit to the pupil and heightens their understanding of how they can become independent learners.

Chapter 4

Are we having any effect?

Penny Manford

The underlying rationale ... is that of enhancing learning with and through texts. At its core is a model of text handling which seeks to enable pupils to become better handlers of text both as readers and writers.

L. Booth 1997: Bid to Standards Fund for
involvement in National Literacy Project KS3

'How are we going to demonstrate that pupils are better "handlers of text"?'

'Standardised tests won't help, they don't assess the relevant skills. I wonder whether they developed any strategies for assessment during the EXEL project? I don't think there's any mention in *Extending Literacy*.'

'Why don't you contact David Wray?'

This chapter tells the story of the resultant action research project carried out, with David Wray's support, in Birmingham LEA (as part of its involvement in the National Literacy Project KS3). The aim was to develop an instrument that would assess pupils' ability in the handling of non-fiction texts. After a brief explanation of the context there will be examination of the problem posed by the need to demonstrate pupil progression as 'handlers of text'. This will be followed with discussion of the process and strategies developed to address this issue. Finally there will be an evaluation of the work so far, with an indication of issues that still need addressing.

The context

Birmingham was one of the 22 LEAs involved in the National Literacy Project KS3 during 1998–9. Schools were invited to bid to participate in the project as part of the Intensive, Medium or Light Touch Programmes. Subsequently 56 schools became involved. The project aimed:

1. To raise standards of literacy at Key Stage 3, especially Year 7.
2. To heighten awareness of the importance of cross-curricular literacy development.
3. To develop strategies/structured approaches to the teaching of literacy skills in all areas of the curriculum.
4. To provide whole-school professional development, focusing on rationale as well as teaching and learning strategies.
5. To support schools' management of literacy.

Our project design was influenced by the belief that literacy development is a whole-school responsibility. This notion is underpinned by the Bullock Report (DES 1975, p. 529) and by HMI findings (DfEE 1997, para. 7) that there is no 'quick fix' solution to deficiencies in literacy and that approaches which involve other curriculum areas in working alongside English are 'more likely to be successful than initiatives confined to English and/or Special Needs departments'. Further support comes from OFSTED inspections which highlight the need for attention to the range of language experiences (written and spoken) and the reading and writing demands throughout the secondary curriculum (Bearne 1999, p. 52). Cross-curricular literacy development had also been identified by DfEE as a key focus for this initiative. Therefore, a major focus for schools on the Intensive Programme was the cross-curricular development of strategies to support pupils in the reading and writing of non-fiction texts. Each curriculum area presents students with a wide range of texts, each of which has its own particular reading style, language and conventional framework, so subject teachers need to share the responsibility for teaching students to understand the text and how to write in the style appropriate to the text model. Research has shown that developing an understanding of different text types, of their characteristic reading and writing demands, increases the confidence and self-esteem of the learner and has a significant effect on his or her performance in all curriculum areas. Thus the EXIT model, which offers a framework for teaching this knowledge, has been central to our professional development programme, although other strategies (such as scaffolded reading experiences (Graves and Graves 1995), DARTs (Lunzer and Gardner 1984), shared and modelled reading and writing (NLS Framework, DfEE 1998c)) have also been drawn upon. The model developed was designed to offer a multi-strategy approach, sufficiently wide to encompass information literacy, on-screen literacy and moving image media;

was informed by Vygotskyan theory; and emphasised the importance of talk, reading and writing in shaping learning.

The problem

We were faced with a major dilemma. How could we demonstrate that this cross-curricular literacy focus was actually making a difference to pupil literacy skill development? What assessment measures could we use that would offer the information that we needed? What did we really want the assessment data to tell us? Was the purpose of the assessment to inform teaching or management or was it for accountability? Clarity of purpose was essential if the assessment was to be properly understood, authentic and informative (Nutbrown 1999, pp. 33–40). Although our prime aim was to inform teaching and learning, there were other considerations. The assessment instrument adopted needed to:

1. *demonstrate progression*, perhaps being sensitive enough to indicate movement from knowledge-telling to knowledge-transforming (Bereiter and Scardamalia 1993);
2. *offer a naturalistic task* that might give evidence of reading and writing as a constructive and interactive process, not a task which simply called for meaning transfer (see Cairney 1990, Wray and Lewis 1997, Mercer 1995), nor a test which lacked authenticity in the tasks presented to pupils (Nutbrown 1999);
3. *be suitable for use by non-language and literacy specialists*, supporting and extending their own developing skills and knowledge of strategies to support pupil literacy development, and encouraging them to see language not only as a means of learning but also as a way of demonstrating learning through 'effective communication' (Bearne 1999, p. 51). If, as Harrison and Salinger (1998 p. xii) suggest, teachers are appropriate agents of assessment, would it be possible to develop a system of classroom-based assessment that would encourage teachers to 'take a closer look' at students' literacy development (as in the Scottish system described by Hayward and Spencer 1998)?

Was such an instrument available? Many assessment procedures have been developed to meet managerial and/or political purposes so it is often the case that they are not well-suited to the immediate purposes of teaching and learning (Stierer 1994, in E825 p. 137). Our need was for an instrument which offered sound theoretical understanding of teaching and learning, and which was something more than a simplistic measure of competence. Standardised reading tests measure only limited aspects of reading behaviour (Merritt 1979, pp. 202–3), not including the ability to handle non-fiction texts. Comprehensive accounts of the development of reading skills (e.g. Beard 1987) make little reference to assessment. There are no standardised tests of writing ability, although the Assessment and Performance Unit (APU) did examine written scripts and debate the relative merits of analytic and impression marking. In other words there was no 'ready-made' asssessment appropriate for our purpose.

A possible solution

The notion of developing an assessment instrument directly linked to the EXIT model arose during discussion with David Wray. He expressed interest in incorporating this into the current phase of EXEL research and has supported us at each phase of development. Such an instrument appeared to offer many advantages. It satisfied three of the basic principles of 'responsive assessment' (Harrison *et al.* 1998, p. 16). Firstly, it switched the emphasis to classroom and curricular practices (two purposes which national programmes are inclined to ignore) by offering assessment evidence that could be of direct value to the teacher and to the student. Secondly, it placed increased emphasis on teacher assessment, while thirdly it offered an opportunity to increase the authenticity of the tasks that formed the basis of the literacy assessment. In addition it offered a structured framework for assessing student interactions with text, could be used to examine performance on a range of genres, built on Littlefair's notion (1991, p. 57) of stages of development of register awareness and heeded Meek's suggestion (1988, p. 38) that student writing can be used as evidence of what they have learnt from their reading. It also raised two of the dilemmas of performance assessment: whether the assessment could be so structured that it would provide teachers with instructionally useful information, and whether it would be possible to develop teacher professional knowledge adequately so that they could use the resulting information effectively and appropriately (Pearson *et al.* 1998 p. 33–6). Since any approach to the assessment of writing is informed by some theory of writing development, of the place of writing in the curriculum and of the way in which writing ought to be promoted in the classroom (Stierer 1994, p. 139), it seemed apposite that the model of assessment adopted should reflect the model of literacy development at the heart of the initiative.

The idea was that subject teachers would devise a baseline task which fitted naturally into their initial programme of study and incorporated as many of the process stages of the EXIT model as possible. The resultant pupil outcomes could then be analysed to produce skill descriptors which were grounded in the data. Progress could be measured by repeating the task at the end of the year using different materials but the same skill descriptors. This would give a robust, quantifiable measure since the number of schools, and therefore of pupils, involved would provide a large database. An added attraction was that involvement in the development of the descriptors would enhance teacher understanding of literacy and of the ways in which they could develop pupil literacy skills within their own subject. A further issue for debate was whether such an assessment framework could also be used to demonstrate transfer of learning. If one member of the project team did not teach the strategies, but set a task at the end of the project in which pupils could demonstrate the research skills they had developed in other subject areas, then the outcome could offer evidence of the extent to which these skills had been internalised and could be drawn upon according to need. This would strengthen the robustness of the model.

The process

Setting the challenge

At the July 1998 conference for teachers from the Intensive Programme schools David Wray posed the question: 'Is what we are doing having an effect on children's learning? How can we know?' He explained that it is possible to check content area learning but not the ability to use texts in those areas, that standardised reading tests take texts out of context and that there are no standardised writing tests. He pointed to the need to demonstrate achievement both quantitatively and qualitatively and suggested that it might be possible to use the EXIT model to provide a framework for examining pupil ability in the reading and writing of non-fiction. For example, if it were possible to adduce criteria to exemplify proficient or poor ability to 'activate prior knowledge', this would provide an evidence-based approach to plotting development. Such a framework would need to be applicable to any subject area, independent of pupil age, and to offer the flexibility to record pupil ability at differing levels for each of the process stages since pupil skill development is not necessarily uniform. The framework suggested was a four-stage grid plotting performance (at emergent, developing, established and advanced levels) against each of the ten process stages. As this was only an embryonic schema there was scope for alternative headings to emerge as teachers interacted with the data to produce the descriptors.

Thus the challenge for teachers was to work in subject groups to devise a naturalistic task that could be used within the subject early in the Autumn term. The task needed to involve interaction with text and to have a clear outcome (although this need not be written). Ideally it would incorporate many, if not all, of the EXIT process stages.

Name:

Figure 4.1 Extending interactions with text – assessment

Process	Emergent	Developing	Established	Advanced
Activation of previous knowledge	Has difficulty in recalling relevant knowledge	Can recall relevant knowledge but has difficulty in applying it	Can recall and apply relevant knowledge	Recalls and applies relevant knowledge in new situations
Establishing purposes	Relies on teacher to set purposes for reading	Can think up purposes for self	Is self-starting and can think of useful approaches to a situation	Thinks of own approaches in new situations
Locating information	Relies on teacher to supply information	Can locate relevant information from a limited choice	Can find own information in an open-ended situation	Looks for information to extend understanding
Adopting appropriate strategies	Has very limited strategies for approaching writing and reading tasks	Has a range of strategies which are used with some confidence	Adopts the most useful strategy according to the situation	Adopts the most useful strategy according to the situation and can depart from it when needed
Interacting with text	Reads the surface of the text but with little evidence of deep understanding	Seeks to understand the text beyond the surface level	Examines own understanding of the text and uses strategies to increase understanding	Conducts an active dialogue with any text including questioning its validity
Monitoring understanding	Has little awareness of areas of non-comprehension	Is aware of areas of non-comprehension and uses strategies to address them	Uses a range of strategies to increase understanding of the text	Can make valid judgements about the comprehensibility of a text
Making a record	Has limited knowledge of ways of recording information from text	Has some strategies for recording information from text	Has a wide range of strategies for recording information from text	Can select the most useful or relevant mode for recording information from text
Evaluating information	Accepts information at face value	Is aware that the information content of a text may be more or less valid for a particular enquiry	Can make reasoned judgements about the value of the information in a given text	Has a wide background knowledge which assists them in making judgements about the value of a text
Assisting memory	Has few or no strageies for conscious learning	Has some strategies for learning which are applied fairly haphazardly	Has a range of strategies for learning which are applied systematically	Can apply a variety of learning strategies in new situations
Communicating information	Has a limited range of forms of expression	Has an awareness of different modes and registers in communicating information	Can employ a wide range of media including IT and non literary media to communicate information	Can employ a wide range of media including IT and non literary media to communicate information according to audience and situation

Key:
(Use a different colour for each assessment and date it)

The Initial Grid

By the start of Day 2 of the Conference the challenge had been grasped and the first draft of an assessment grid produced. One of the school Literacy Project leaders (Ken Bonham) appeared with a grid containing the descriptors for all ten process stages at each of the four levels. Copies were produced for all schools and confidence in the ability to develop appropriate tasks grew. After some alteration by David Wray the format 'Extending interactions with text – assessment' (see Figure 4.1) was adopted.

Developing baseline tasks

Project schools demonstrated their creativity as they produced baseline tasks which matched their own curricular needs and teaching styles. As Figure 4.2 'Assessing non-fiction skills: analysis of baseline tasks and pupil scripts' demonstrates, these tasks varied not only in content but also in their length, the range of demands placed on pupils and the extent of teacher support. Closer examination of some individual school examples illustrates this variation in response more effectively.

Example 1: 'Catching them early'

Development of the baseline task in one Geography department was guided by the belief that the task should be completed early, as part of the introduction to the first programme of study, and with minimal teacher intervention. Having produced an outline for the task, the Project Team (a member of SMT, the SENCO and the Head of Humanities) realised that it only offered opportunity for pupils to demonstrate achievement in four of the EXIT process stages. They were also concerned to assess pupil ability on the more secretarial aspects of writing. After discussion with the Literacy Consultant a solution emerged – to produce a version of the grid which included only those elements. In this grid (see Figure 4.3, page 59) the descriptors for the activation of previous knowledge, adopting appropriate strategies and interacting with text were adapted, while those for communicating information were rewritten to assess aspects of the written outcome more explicitly.

Example 2: 'Observing performance'

Sheeran and Barnes 1991 (p. 40) suggest that even with the advent of records of achievement which place more emphasis on oral skills and practical abilities, written work is likely to retain its primacy in most schemes of assessment. Although this statement reflected the situation in many project schools there was awareness of the importance of listening to pupils to gain evidence of the strategies they employed.

Baseline data in School C (see Figure 4.2) was designed to draw on work completed in two subjects (English and History) as part of the LEA Transition Module 'Moving On Up'. The tasks offered the opportunity for pupils to demonstrate achievement in six of the EXIT process stages. It was felt that to ensure

Figure 4.2   Assessing non-fiction skills – analysis of baseline tasks and pupil scripts

School	Subject(s)	Task outline	EXIT process stages	Comments
A	English	*'Last of the Mohicans'* • Make notes about life of author (James Fenimore Cooper). • Story summary – KWL grid.	1, 2, 3, 4, 5, 6, 7, 10	• Photographic and textual evidence. • Developed system of grading pupils at three levels within each stage to demonstrate security of achieving criteria. • Introduced 'pre-emergent' stage.
	History	• Wanted poster. • Brainstorm.		
B	Geography History Literacy	*'Moving On Up'* – *History of Birmingham's Canals; Development of Brindley Place* • Debate. • Radio script – news item on the debate. • Brochure to promote Brindley Place.	1, 2, 3, 4, 5, 7, 8, 10	• Nine lesson module taught across the three departments. • Included text marking, use of grid to develop knowledge of unfamiliar vocabulary, writing frame as role preparation for debate, grid to assist note-taking. • Great effort put into production of brochures.
C	English History	*'Moving On Up'* – *Betsy Grimes, Recipes* • Analysis and production of procedural text. • Text marking. • QUADS grid.	1, 2, 3, 5, 7, 10	• Tasks completed during September. • Grid produced to match each task. • Some assessment via observation, using collaborative teacher.
D	Science	*'How to use a thermometer'* • Brainstorm. • Text marking. • Writing description and explanation.	1, 2, 4, 5, 6, 10	• Task completed late September. • Lesson plan produced for all staff to standardise approach. • Marking scale produced, assessing factual content. • Topic introduced via teacher input followed by pupils completing brainstorm individually and unsupported. • Text read to pupils by teacher. • Teacher modelling of use of thermometer. • Summary sheet produced.

consistency in assessing work the descriptors needed to offer more detailed criteria for pupil performance. New descriptors were written, but then a new problem emerged: the written script would not offer evidence of achievement in all these facets. The solution – observation. One member of the team could work alongside the subject teacher, observe the focus pupils and record their achievement. This necessitated slight adaptation to the grid's format so that it could be used to record the outcomes of both observation and the analysis of the written outcome.

Figure 4.3   Assessing text use in geography

A. Initial Task – Geography of the Local Area

Introduction to the idea of the geography of the local area. Brainstorming of students' geographical knowledge and terms already known and understood by them; some words on board. Examine Birmingham map to locate area and discuss aerial photograph of the area.

Task: Outline and describe the geography of the local area.

An extended piece of individual written work with no further teacher intervention. Students encouraged to support their ideas with drawings/sketches.

A note to be kept of the time taken to produce the finished product. Completed work to be kept on file in order that progress can be measured.

B. Assessment focus points

Process	Assessment comments
1. Activation of previous knowledge	
2. Adopting appropriate strategies	
3. Interacting with text	
4. Communicating information	
4.1 Spelling	
4.2 Legibility	
4.3 Grammar	

Example 3: 'Where Birmingham People Live'

In order to ensure that the baseline task offered appropriate opportunities for pupils to demonstrate achievement in the different process stages one school produced a task outline which mapped the relationship between the tasks and the EXIT model (see Figure 4.4 overleaf). The Assessment Grid (Figure 4.1, page 56) could then be used to record pupil performance.

Example 4: 'Making a Pencil Case'

Some tasks were designed to gather evidence over a period of time. In one school Y7 Technology is taught as seven-week modules. EXIT strategies were used at intervals throughout the Textiles module 'Making a Pencil Case'. A brainstorm was used to activate prior knowledge and to establish needs for the design specification. This was followed by a sequencing activity to guide planning. Finally, pupil written evaluation of their product was supported by a writing frame. All this pupil work was examined in order to complete the assessment grid.

Example 5: 'Elements of Music'

As Figure 4.2 shows, some schools sought to collect data from more than one curriculum area in order to produce a broader evidence base on which to make judgement of individual achievement. Teachers from Music, History and English worked together to identify the skills which they believed pupils needed to develop and the aspects of the EXIT model which addressed these. Tasks were designed which would demonstrate initial performance and three grids designed – the first mapping the

Figure 4.4 A school's task outline mapping the relationship between the tasks and the EXIT model

---

Non-fiction Assessment Task

Subject: Geography
Target Group: All Y7 pupils will complete tasks, scripts of nine pupils will be analysed in detail.
Topic: Where Birmingham People Live (Unit 3 in the Transition Module 'Moving On Up').

Pupil tasks linked to stages within the EXIT model:
1. Activating prior knowledge:
   KWL grid, first column 'What I know about where different ethnic groups live in Birmingham'.
2. Establishing purpose:
   KWL grid, second column 'What I want to find out about where Birmingham people live'.
3. Interacting with text:
   Reading source material 'Where do people of different ethnic groups live in Birmingham' and examining the map.
4. Locating information:
   Identifying other sources of information, e.g. asking parents, other teachers; using library.
5. Monitoring understanding:
   Asking questions about the text.
6. Making a record:
   Making notes of the information by completing KWL grid, column 3.
7. Communicating information.
8. Using a writing frame to structure an explanation of where people live in Birmingham.

Pupils will complete tasks on A4 paper.

If possible, observational notes will be made of the way in which the focus group approach non-written stages.

Note. Similar tasks will also be completed in History and RE so that a broader evidence base will be available for assessing each individual pupil's skills.

---

relationship between the school and the EXIT criteria and the others representing subject-specific adaptations.

The Music assessment was conducted in October, after the completion of practical assessment. It included the activation of prior knowledge using a brainstorm, interaction with text through research, report writing and evaluation. Pupil performance was recorded on a subject-specific grid which differed from that used in all other schools in that there was space to make specific comment in addition to highlighting the appropriate descriptors.

Sharing practice and assigning levels

In October, at another conference for schools in the Intensive Programme, school project teams met to examine their developing practice in the assessment of non-fiction text-handling skills, being encouraged to engage in critical reflection on the use of the EXIT model for this purpose. Schools shared the tasks which they had designed as a baseline, commenting on the feasibility of using the EXIT model both to structure these and to collect evidence of the different processes involved therein. David Wray introduced the session by explaining the structure of the assessment grid, stressing the need to develop consistency in the understanding and application of the terminology. He also suggested the importance of contextualising each assessment by giving a brief outline of the task and the date of completion. This information could be appended to the grid. Subsequent assessments could be dated with descriptors highlighted in a different colour. Staff then worked together to examine the scripts of the nine pupils in their focus group, attempting to match them to the EXIT Assessment Framework and to develop a shared understanding of the four levels of attainment.

Target-setting

Once the individual pupil grids had been highlighted it was possible to identify the 'best-fit' level for the pupil's current level of achievement. This data was used to set the target for improvement and was included as a quantitative measure of school performance, as in the following example:

> *Target:* To increase pupil ability in the handling of non-fiction texts from a position where 5 of the focus group are at Emergent level and 4 at Developing level to a position where there are 2 at Emergent level, 5 at Developing level and 2 at Established level.

Demonstrating progression

Reassessment was planned for the latter half of the Summer term. Schools would devise a second task, again matched to the current programme of study and which revisited the same elements of the EXIT model. Scripts were to be analysed and the grids updated – only then would we be able to judge the effectiveness of the focus on non-fiction text-handling and of the grid as a means to demonstrate this progression.

Evaluating the framework

Key questions

Our initial evaluation of the framework attempted to address the following questions:

- Is the framework applicable to the assessment of non-fiction text-handling skills?

- Can it be made applicable by teachers?
- Does it offer appropriate flexibility in use?
- Can it be used over time to demonstrate progression in a way which is both meaningful to teachers and helpful in terms of structuring or developing pupil learning?

What the teachers said

Teacher comments suggested a range of positive outcomes:

- The framework not only provides diagnostic information of individual pupil strengths and weaknesses, but its structure also facilitates identification of appropriate teaching strategies to develop individual skills. *'This is what they can do and this is what I am going to do to develop their skills. Therefore it informs my planning and teaching.'*
- The framework offers a useful model for formative assessment. Other tests, e.g. standardised reading tests, can be used to give quantitative measures. *'This is useful to help pupils on.'* *'The grid is brilliant as a formative tool to demonstrate levels of cognitive development.'*
- It offers useful qualitative data. *'The most important aspect is what it does for pupils.'*
- The model offers a wider picture of pupil skills than the tests normally used for value-added purposes.
- Completion of grids for a group of pupils serves to highlight teaching strategies which are insufficiently represented within the teacher's repertoire.
- Use of the grid supports professional development. Teachers valued the opportunity it afforded of working with colleagues to examine strategies and share different interpretations of the task in order to develop personal understanding and expertise.

These comments not only reflect Czerniewska's view (1992, p. 158) that the knowledge of language development desired by teachers goes far beyond 'spelling rules and grammatical niceties' to information about how pupils respond to a range of reading and writing experiences, but also demonstrates that such assessment is important to enhance professional expertise and to inform teaching and learning.

The grid was also seen to have potential as a tool for school self-evaluation and improvement. It was suggested that if the grid were used by more than one subject (as it has been in some schools), it is possible that the same pupil would be attributed a different profile for each subject. Examination as to why the pupil demonstrated these strengths differentially would not only reveal greater information about individual learning styles but would also offer scope for analysing departmental teaching practice and emphases.

There were also some reservations about the use of the Framework, particularly at this stage in its development. It was accepted that to be effective there was a need for the baseline assessment to encompass a number of tasks since one task was unlikely to offer evidence on the full range of process stages. It was also felt that there was an issue with respect to teacher unfamiliarity with the teaching approach within the EXIT model. One teacher commented that there was a 'low staff skills base in terms of developing these skills' and that judgments might therefore be unreliable, inconsistent or unrepresentative of the levels pupils were actually capable of achieving. Finally there was a feeling that the 'emergent' statements needed to be written in more positive language to represent what pupils are able to do. (This criticism was immediately addressed by Ken Bonham and his reworked draft of the Assessment Grid can be seen in Figure 4.5, overleaf.)

What did it tell us about pupil performance?

The value of any assessment framework lies in its ability to offer data which both indicates current performance levels and sets the agenda for future development. The role which the EXIT Assessment Framework can play in this respect is exemplified by the following extract from one school's evaluation of pupil response to the baseline assessment.

Example 6: Examining Aspects of Japanese Life
The task comprised the use of brainstorm and concept-mapping to establish the precise purpose for research into an aspect of Japanese life. After conducting research pupils made presentations to their class. Evidence of the outcomes exists in the form of photographs, videotape, written reports and posters.

Some pupils, who grasped the idea of the KWFL grid, produced a presentation which was interesting, clear, related to their 'Want to Know' questions and reflected a sound understanding of the assessment criteria, and produced writing which was well-structured and thoughtful, needed to have experience of using a wider range of texts and making more reasoned judgements about the value of information in a given text in order to move them from 'Developing' to 'Established' level.

Pupils who had grasped the concept of the KWFL grid but concentrated too hard on the presentation at the expense of the quality of their pieces of writing needed instruction to develop their awareness of different modes and registers in communicating information in order to consolidate their performance at 'Developing' level.

Pupils who abandoned their KWFL grid, lost sight of their key question and resorted to wholesale copying of texts with a resulting loss of understanding and relevance needed guidance in establishing purposes, strategies for interacting with the text at more than surface level and for recording information to move them beyond 'Emergent' level.

Figure 4.5 Extending interactions with text – assessment, revised version

Name:

Process	Emergent	Developing	Established	Advanced	Teaching
Activation of previous knowledge *What do I already know?*	Can recall some relevant information	Can recall relevant information but has difficulty in applying it	Can recall and apply relevant information	Recalls and applies relevant information in new situations	• Brainstorm • Concept map • KWL
Establishing purposes *What do I want to find out?*	Responds to reading tasks set by teacher	Can think up tasks for self	Is self-starting and can think of useful approaches to a situation	Thinks of own approaches in new situations	• Questioning • KWL/QUADS
Locating information *Where will I find it?*	Can use information supplied by teacher	Can locate relevant information from a limited choice	Can find own information in an open ended situation	Looks for information to extend their understanding	• Contextualise • Library skills
Adopting appropriate strategies *How should I use it?*	Has a few strategies for approaching writing and reading tasks	Has a range of strategies that they can use with some confidence	Adopts the most useful strategy according to the situation	Adopts a useful or challenging strategy from a range according to the situation	• Metacognition • Modelling
Interacting with text *What can I do to improve my understanding?*	Reads the surface of the text	Seeks to understand and ask questions of the text	Examines own understanding of the text and uses strategies to increase their understanding	Conducts a dialogue with any text including questioning its validity for the purpose	• DARTS • Text marking • Text restructuring • Genre exchange

Process	Emergent	Developing	Established	Advanced	Teaching
Monitoring understanding *What can I do about the bits I don't understand?*	Has a little awareness of areas of non-comprehension	Is aware of areas of non-comprehension and uses strategies to address them	Uses a range of strategies to increase their understanding of the text	Can make valid judgements about the relevance, validity and comprehensibility of a text	• Modelling • Strategy charts • Grids
Making a record *What should I make note of in this information?*	Can record some information from text	Has a few skills for recording information from text	Has a wide range of strategies for recording information from text	Can select the most useful or relevant mode for recording information from text	• Modelling • Writing frames • Grids
Evaluating information *Should I believe this information? How can I check it?*	Accepts information at face value or is unaware of the information content of a text	Is aware of the information content of a text and that it may be more or less valid for a particular enquiry	Can make reasoned judgements about the value of the information in a given text	Has a wide background knowledge which assists them in making judgements about the value of a text	• Modelling • Discussion of biased texts
Assisting memory *How can I help myself remember the important parts?*	Has started to learn consciously	Has learnt some strategies for learning and started to use them	Has a range of strategies for learning which are applied systematically	Can apply a variety of learning strategies in new situations	• Revisit • Review • Restructure
Communicating information *How should I tell other people?*	Can express ideas in more than one mode	Has an awareness of different modes and registers in communicating information	Can employ a wide range of media including IT and non-literary media to communicate information	Can employ a wide range of media including IT and non-literary media to communicate information according to audience and situation	• Using a range of genres • Writing frames • Publishing • Alternatives

Key:
(Use a different colour for each assessment and date it)

Such information, used in conjunction with EXIT teaching strategies, could be used to set targets for pupil learning and to determine an appropriate teaching programme.

Issues arising

The EXIT Assessment Framework is one attempt to respond to Stierer's call (1994, p. 138) for imaginative thinking 'to develop reading assessment procedures capable of discriminating more dynamically between individual readers than the national assessment scale does' and exceeds it to the extent to which it also incorporates assessment of the ability to communicate information in the written form. However there are issues which need to be addressed before it becomes the robust and comprehensive measure we seek.

Firstly, there needs to be greater consistency of approach. There is need for a common understanding of the concept 'baseline testing', with consistent levels of support for pupils in different schools if the data is to have more than internal validity. In order to permit comparison across schools there also needs to be an agreed time for the assessment to be conducted. Schools carried out assessments at different stages in the term – the later the baseline data was collected the more pupils might have been influenced by the teaching which had taken place.

Secondly, there needs to be a careful revision of the level descriptors in the light of experience. Some do not seem to describe progression in a sufficiently discriminating way or are open to misinterpretation. The end-of-year assessment should offer an opportunity to address this issue.

Thirdly, there is need for consideration of the extent to which the assessments are actually used to inform teaching and learning and whether the data is meaningful to teachers who have not been involved in the initiative. It would also be interesting to examine pupil texts produced in subjects where the teacher has not been involved to see whether pupils are actually able to transfer skills in the handling of non-fiction texts without explicit prompt. That perhaps would offer an indicative measure of the success of our whole KS3 Literacy Project.

The next challenge? To revise and refine the Framework in the light of experience and then to encourage other schools and teachers within the city to adopt it as an integral part of their drive to raise standards of achievement in literacy.

Acknowledgement

The success of this initiative is due to the hard work, creativity and commitment of the Literacy Project Teams in the Intensive Programme schools. Particular thanks are due to K. Bonham, L. Booth, J. Clark, C. Close, D. Dawson, B. Elgar, D. Fellowes, M. Gales, W. Magna, T. Quinn, A. Ridge, S. Simpson, L. Timoney and D. Williams for allowing their work to be used to illustrate and exemplify the developments.

Chapter 5

Making sense of the world: language and learning in Geography

Douglas Greig

> The limits of my language mean the limits of my world.
> (Wittgenstein 1922: p. 149)

> Thought undergoes many changes as it turns into speech. It does not merely find expression in speech; it finds reality and form.
> (Vygotsky 1986)

The quotations above underpin my approach to teaching and learning. This approach gives rise to the techniques and strategies that will be described in this chapter. I will provide an overview of a series of Geography lessons and materials that focus both on the process of learning and the vital role of language within it. Written and spoken language is developed within these lessons as a means of learning, not just an outcome. Such an approach can address two concerns. First, a concern to improve the learning of Geography across Key Stages 3, 4 and 5. Second, the need to promote the effective development of the skills of reading, writing, speaking and listening across the curriculum of a secondary school in order to better prepare students for the increasing demands upon their literacy skills as they progress through and beyond the education system. This approach does not ignore the important knowledge, understanding and skills that are a pivotal component of any subject. Rather, the techniques and resources outlined will demonstrate how these discrete elements of a subject can become a vehicle for the development of literacy skills. It will show how an explicit focus on supporting and scaffolding children's reading and writing can improve their performance as geographers – or practitioners of any subject.

How people learn

Before describing the lessons, I will begin with a brief look at some key learning principles because it is important that we reflect upon the way that people learn and hence on how this process can be improved. An important first principle is that children are not passive receivers of knowledge. Much of current theory about how people learn demonstrates how individuals actively engage with the world that surrounds them in an effort to make sense of it, by bringing some form of meaning to any given situation (Hanley 1994; Leat 1997; Wells 1987; Wray and Lewis 1997). Learning emerges from this process as people adapt previously formed ideas and concepts in the light of new experiences and evidence. People try to understand new ideas and material by interpreting them through existing knowledge structures. In this way, meaning and learning are intimately connected to experience. Therefore, if learning is to be effective and long-lasting it must use this process actively. Memorised facts or information that have not been connected with the learner's prior understanding will quickly be forgotten or become redundant (Hanley 1994). The techniques and strategies presented in this chapter thus aim to activate and engage prior knowledge in order to enhance the learning that takes place. Literacy cannot be divorced from this process.

Language is the most common medium through which teachers and pupils transact their business. Given this, Wittgenstein's point about the restrictive effect of limited language has important implications for teachers. In order to make children's learning more effective a teacher must look at how a child's world can be expanded through a focus on how their language skills develop. In fact, teaching must appreciate that the understanding people have of the world around them is constructed from language. When such an understanding is translated into classroom practice it will promote an improvement in children's knowledge and understanding of a subject and their level of literacy. Effective teaching should be about facilitating the expansion of these limits, and equipping an individual with the tools to be able to carry out this expansion for themselves. Therefore, the literacy skills of each pupil are essential tools and not an accidental outcome in the process of learning, and it is vital that their use and development should be carefully planned for.

Talking and writing to learn

The much-used phrase 'talking and writing to learn' encapsulates much of the ideas outlined above. The tasks that pupils are set in a classroom should incorporate the structured use of language as a means of learning. Moreover, this learning is often more effective if it is placed into a social context. The work of a pair or a group activates the need for oral communication that stimulates the crucial processes

Vygotsky mentions. The role of spoken language and discussion is important in helping to develop new concepts as it forces children to speculate and negotiate with each other about the material in front of them. It therefore places them in the position of being able to make sense of the new material by making connections with previously held ideas, and to empower them to make generalisations and develop new understanding. This is the foundation of making learning more effective and more transferable.

The essential outcome of such beliefs is that literacy needs to be considered as an intrinsic part of every subject because this allows teachers to make learning more effective. This does not involve breaking the development of literacy down into a series of measurable steps and skills. Rather it necessitates a focus on the overlapping and interdependent processes that help to develop and construct the literacies of specific areas of the curriculum. This means we must examine how literacy is harnessed and used within our discrete curriculum areas and also consider how effective literacy development can be planned and delivered through our subjects. Above all, the work which will be described in this chapter looks at ideas and concepts that are common to many of the subjects that make up the school curriculum. These include the practices of listening, categorising, information seeking, problem-solving, recording, analysing, communicating, reflecting and planning (Webster *et al.* 1996, Leat 1998).

From theory into practice

We will now see how these theories can be applied in a real school situation and how it can make a difference, by examining part of a Year 8 course on 'Rivers' delivered by the Geography department in a mixed comprehensive school located in the London Borough of Greenwich. The Year 8 class that features in this account was a mixed ability class of 30 students with reading ages ranging from 7.3 years to 13.2 years. It was a class that did not have a reputation for being calm and passive – rather the opposite.

The Bangladesh floods of 1998

As part of the National Curriculum in Geography schools are required to teach students at Key Stage 3 about the causes and responses to flooding. In 1998 a disastrous series of floods struck the less developed country of Bangladesh, covering over 75 per cent of the country including the capital Dhaka. Whilst thinking about using the Bangladesh floods as a case study for this topic, I discovered a wealth of resources such as newspaper articles, eyewitness accounts, video and photographic resources on the Internet. These formed the factual and real basis of this topic, demonstrating the Internet's worth as an educational resource.

The floods are a topic rich in both content and skills. Many areas of the National Curriculum in Geography are covered. As well as the content of river flooding within the context of a contrasting locality, it facilitates consideration of a variety of broader understanding and skills:

(a) it allows consideration of the 'big ideas' of cause and effect (Leat 1998);
(b) through the nature of the tasks the students develop their skills in classifying information and in carrying out research;
(c) students begin to analyse the decision-making processes that people go through prior to making life changing moves, and the role of social status and economic power within this;
(d) students also have the opportunity to move on to assess the role of economic development in governing the impact of such a natural disaster and they can weigh up solutions that might be put in place to sustainably manage the drainage basin of the River Ganges in order to reduce the risk of flooding.

The model shown in Figure 5.1 summarises the main elements of the teaching and learning processes within this topic but it is not meant to be a generic model to be applied in all situations.

The 'route of enquiry' that it demonstrates is crucial to understanding how Geography can effectively address issues of attainment and literacy. This is founded on the belief that to improve the learning that takes place in the classroom it is necessary to incorporate and use children's sense of wonder about the world around them. This wonder is best stimulated by real life events, probing questions and challenging tasks. Furthermore, the model points to a shift in the role of the teacher towards one of a facilitator and mediator, who can debrief effectively to draw out new points of learning. This is a role that is much less secure and predictable than the role of the teacher as the 'sole expert'.

What follows is a worked example of this model. This is in three phases that correspond to the different stages involved in the evolution of the final written report. The work has been influenced by my collaborative work with the London Borough of Greenwich Secondary Literacy Advisor (see Chapter 10 of this book), the work of the EXEL project (Wray and Lewis 1997) and, importantly, by the 'Thinking Through Geography Group' (TTG), based at the University of Newcastle. This group developed resources and strategies in order to address issues of challenge, transfer of skills, and the raising of attainment in Geography (Leat 1998) and many of the strategies used in the lessons were first demonstrated by this group.

Figure 5.1 A model of the teaching and learning processes and their link with literacy

Stage of learning	Key questions	Teaching strategy used	Literacy element
Activating prior knowledge	What do I already know about Bangladesh? What do I already know about rivers and flooding?	• Brainstorming in pairs to produce a spider diagram or list.	• Discussion of prior knowledge – establishing links between new and old sets of learning.
Familiarising with a new topic	What are the main events?	• Storytelling. • Picture boarding.	• Listening and writing notes. • Making decisions about relevant and irrelevant material. • Applying knowledge to visual stimulus and generating a written response.
Selecting a learning strategy	What am I trying to find out? What are the relevant points to pick out of this material? Can I find any categories in this material? How can these categories improve how I use this material?	• Deciding on relevant and important material. • Oral discussion. • Sorting cards and ideas (mystery game). • Debriefing led by teacher.	• Speaking to different groups of people for different purposes – speculating, negotiating, presenting ideas. • Listening to others' views. • Reading material and categorising it.
Making a record	What do I need to record to answer the task? How should I record these ideas?	• Writing lists and thoughts in different stages. • A structured note-taking frame.	• Writing down relevant material – making notes.
Reformulating ideas and strategies	Do I have all the material I need to come to an answer? Can I apply any other ideas to this material? Is there any other relevant material that I need or have that could be useful in answering the task? What do other people think? What are the intentions of the author? Who was this text written for? Is there any bias in any of this material?	• Sorting activity (mystery game). • Debriefing led by teacher. • Drafting of work. • Students marking own and other people's work.	• Speaking – speculating and negotiating. • Reading and re-reading material to re-work ideas, and apply new concepts. • Writing – drafting and marking of work.
Making generalisations	What are my thoughts and findings about the question or task?	• Oral discussion. • Debriefing led by teacher. • Oral presentation. • Written presentation.	• Speaking to a wider audience using specific vocabulary. • Writing an extended explanatory account. • Writing for a particular purpose to a specific audience.
Communicating conclusions	How am I going to present my findings? Who am I presenting my findings to? How should I structure my presentation? What vocabulary should I use?	• Oral presentation by students. • Debriefing led by teacher. • Written presentation. • Writing frames.	• Speaking to a wider audience using specific vocabulary. • Writing an extended explanatory account. • Writing for a particular purpose to a specific audience. • Writing – drafting and marking of work.

(Note: this model does not necessarily work in a linear fashion, and each stage can take place over a series of lessons as well as in a single lesson.)

Phase 1 Mustafa's Story

This first lesson used a strategy called 'story-telling' (Leat 1998) in order to familiarise the students with the location and events surrounding the flooding. Stories are an excellent means of stimulating wonder and interest, but are often underused by teachers in secondary schools. An extract from the story is shown in Figure 5.2, and the lesson itself lasted one hour.

Mustafa's Story

Mustafa woke up early on the Tuesday morning, in time to get himself ready for school. He knows he's lucky as none of his other brothers and sisters are going to school at the moment, but at the same time he always wishes he didn't have to get up so early. His school is about two miles away from his home across the flat flood plain of the River Ganges. Bangladesh, where Mustafa lives, is a very flat place as it is mostly made up of the delta of three rivers. That's the area of land that the rivers make when they reach the sea and dump off the mud and silt that they are carrying because they slow down in the ocean. Gradually this dumped material builds up into new land, and is why most of Mustafa's country is under 100 metres high.

It had been raining for three days. In fact, since April, it had rained much more than it usually would, and it had got really bad since the rainy season started in June. Now in September, all of this rain meant that the rivers and streams near where Mustafa lived were really full and some had flooded. Mustafa hated the rain. It meant his walk to school would be uncomfortable and that he and his friends wouldn't be able to play outside.

He switched on the radio to try and find something to listen to while he got ready. All of a sudden he heard a lady's voice as he was turning the dial. She was speaking quite quickly and in the background you could hear lots of people moving, shouting and screaming. The lady continued to speak.

'I'm here in Mirpur a district of Dhaka our capital city. I'm standing on one of the only roads out of the city that is left open as hundreds and thousands of people run away from the flood waters that are covering the land and buildings in Mirpur.

To date 75 per cent of Bangladesh is under the flood water. Thirty thousand villages have disappeared or been destroyed. Thirty million people have been left homeless. On top of this people rely on the land to grow food and to earn a living. With one million hectares of land under water, most of the farming has had to stop because the crops and animals are often drowned under the water. This also means that many thousands of people are in danger of losing their only way of earning a living.'

Figure 5.2   Extract from Mustafa's story

The students' task was to write down (in their draft books) any important details and events they heard while the story was being read out. The teacher then gathered together ideas on a board, modelling some of the important information. The class was asked to reflect upon whether any of these details had things in common, and whether they could be grouped together. Unprompted suggestions included causes, effects, problems, people, nature and weather.

The teacher then asked students to reflect on how they decided to write something down, and how they actually recorded it. This stimulated a discussion led by the teacher asking open questions about how people can develop their learning and thinking. Examples would be:

- What did you find easy to write down?
- Why was it easy to write down?
- What made you think something was important?
- How did you decide what to write down?
- As you were listening did anything make it difficult to write something down?
- How could you improve how you wrote things down in the future?

This debriefing session is consolidating not only the content that has been covered, but also the process of getting that information. Thus, it is helping students to appreciate what they have done to carry out the task. This is what some authors have described as metacognition (thinking about thinking) – a crucial element of creating independent and literate learners (Leat 1997, 1998, Wray and Lewis 1997). The story was read out for a final time and the students applied these new categories and techniques to the same information.

The homework from this lesson was to take ten pictures photographed during the flood and to write a sentence next to each one describing what was shown. The aim was to consolidate what they had covered in the content of the lesson and to use the skill of breaking down the events into different categories. These photographs and the sentences the students individually generated would form the beginning of the written work done in Phase 3. The homework provided an initial record of the children's impression of the floods. This first phase of the enquiry provided an opportunity for students to make links between their previous knowledge and understanding with the new material so as to construct a new set of learning. However, it also equipped them with an understanding of how they can perform this process for themselves by making the learning process explicit.

Phase 2 A Mystery Game

This is another strategy that the TTG group have demonstrated to good effect, and one which is commonly known to many geographers through the Kobe earthquake activity that SCAA published as an exemplar assessment task for Key Stage 3

Geography. However, the game developed here is unique in its content and the questions that are posed. Mystery games are literally what they say. They are games in which a pair or group of students try to solve a 'mysterious' question. They are a sophisticated form of sorting activity comprising several general elements:

- a central 'open' question which needs to be solved;
- a real context in which this question can be posed;
- information presented on between 16 to 30 cards that can be physically manipulated and moved around;
- some narrative element to the mystery;
- names of people and places that lend a 'story' to the events: this is particularly important at Key Stage 3;
- a classroom set up that fosters group and pair work: rows of singular or paired tables are not conducive to the success of this sort of activity.

(after Leat, 1998)

The 'mystery' given was to discover which of two families, living in Dhaka at the time of the flood, moved away and the reasons for the move.

The class was split into pairs, and each pair was given the cards in an envelope, as well as a recording frame that is shown in Figure 5.3. They were introduced to the aims and expectations of the lesson, before moving into a carefully structured programme of learning activities. The seven point plan below summarises this structure.

1. The students were set the 'mystery' with a clear emphasis that it was not only the 'answer' that was required but also the reasons why.
2. They spread the cards and split them into two piles after deciding which of the cards helped them answer the question and which did not. They were then given some time to write down their first thoughts about the issue using the recording frame.
3. Next they were asked for contributions about the answers they had come up with so far. This strategy is used to move from paired oral work into a whole-class discussion. This was an important element of the lesson as the teacher acts as a mediator, debriefing them about their thinking and progress through the task. Some of these thoughts were recorded on the board.
4. They were then asked to consider whether they could categorise any of the ideas that they had come up with so far and given about five minutes to do this. Contributions were again requested and recorded.
5. The next stage was to re-work their original conclusions in the light of steps 3 and 4. These new thoughts were noted down on their writing frame.
6. The penultimate step was to generate a final conclusion in their pairs incorporating all of their thinking about the mystery question. These were delivered as oral presentations at the start of the next lesson.

There are two families to look at in this mystery. The Hossain family and the Chowdury family, who both live in Dhaka, the capital of Bangladesh. Four days after the floods began, one of these families had to leave their home and move away. Your task is to find out who decided to move and why this happened.

Names: _____

First thoughts and findings:

_____
_____
_____
_____
_____
_____
_____

Further thoughts and findings:

_____
_____
_____
_____
_____
_____
_____

Conclusion:

_____
_____
_____
_____
_____

Figure 5.3 Recording frame for mystery game

7. Finally they reflected upon the methods and learning that had gone on. This was again done via open questions from the teacher such as 'How did talking help you?'; 'What strategies did you use that helped you come up with that conclusion?'; 'What was tricky about this task?'

This task was completed in an hour-long lesson and the students' final categories included climate, nature, people, towns, land, income, food, disease and water in the fifth part of the lesson.

This session demonstrated how students were actively involved in the manipulation of the material through what they already understood and how this understanding was expanded through oral interaction with the teacher and a partner. This task was rich in its use and development of literacy skills. First, oral work played a central function in the activity and involved the students actively manipulating the text to come up with 'meaning'. As they were in a pair they had to speculate and negotiate about the outcome. Where there was conflict they had to develop skills in compromising and solving disagreements. The format of the text as small 'bites' and ones which could be moved around, allowed ideas to be tested out, re-worked and links to be drawn between different parts of the material. It allowed a text that as a whole would have been far too complex and intimidating for most of these students, to become a vehicle by which they developed a sophisticated understanding of Geography. In fact their use and manipulation of the text in this way placed them in the position of being able to use it actively to develop their thinking. By grouping different aspects together and drawing links between them, they were actively reading the text and building a new understanding. The debriefing that took place at key moments in the lesson was crucial to developing their understanding and their use of the text. The teacher had to be open and responsive to the comments from the students, and had carefully to guide and channel their thinking towards a clearer understanding. This can be a very successful way to support them in reflecting about how they have read and understood the text, thus moving their literacy skills on.

There are other important facets that contributed to the success of this activity. The structure and pacing of the lesson separated the processes of reading and writing so that it was not just a matter of 'comprehension testing'. The written work demanded that they applied the reading and re-reading they had done to a particular key question to generate their conclusion. The learning took place as they continuously reflected on their answer and how the text could help them to solve the mystery. This and the previous phase were also rich in their use of all the senses (except smell) to stimulate the wonder that many of the students had, even those to whom text was normally a barrier to understanding. In fact the multi-sensory learning environment that Phases 1 and 2 created was rewarding for both the students and the teacher.

Phase 3 Why did the 1998 Flood in Bangladesh have such a big effect?

An important facet of teaching is to broaden and open up the limits of a student's current thinking. That is why this last stage did not simply repeat the question covered in the mystery game itself. The students now had to consider the impact at the level of a country rather than a family, which demanded that they applied their thinking about the issue to a new context. This extended their thought processes and also forced them to reconsider their current conclusion. The fundamental objective of this task was that each individual student would produce an extended piece of written work. Importantly this would be assessed as part of the portfolio of work that each student in the school produced for their Key Stage 3 assessment in Geography. However, another important aspect of this was to produce a written conclusion about a complex issue that put over a particular point of view, using a register that was appropriate to the audience, and a format that fulfilled the brief that the students had been given. The written task was itself therefore an important aspect of extending each student's literacy skills as it demanded consideration of register and audience as well as the content of the written answer. The format of the task was chosen to both challenge and interest the students. Their task was to produce a 'documentary' about the floods, which must answer the overall question, 'Why did the floods of 1998 have such a big effect in Bangladesh?' They were given the ten photographs from the homework in Phase 1, of which they had to use at least eight. Each photograph had to represent a different screen shot, and had to be accompanied by a written paragraph(s) that provided the commentary to accompany the picture. The nature of the task thus meant that the students had to consider some important issues in producing their answer:

- The evidence and material they would use.
- How they would use it.
- The structure and flow of their writing.
- The conclusion that they would draw, and how this would be built up by the structure. The use of the photographs, so that they tied in and told the story pictorially.
- The use of an impersonal and formal register that can be associated with scientific and explanatory genres of writing.
- The use of subject-specific vocabulary.

These elements demanded the development of literacy skills that went beyond the skill of physically writing, and moved it to a more challenging level, and one which was richer as a learning experience. As such the task was given a huge priority in terms of time, and following our departmental policy, would be written in draft before being produced in a final version. The first stage was to take the ten photographs, decide which ones to use, and then to place them in an order that would allow the development of a conclusion. This permitted those who found the task of writing from scratch difficult, the opportunity to develop a plan using a visual stimulus. Their access to the task was therefore enhanced.

Important resources in this written work were the writing frames that were produced to support the students in making some of the difficult decisions listed above. They were produced at two levels. The first was heavily structured and included prompts to scaffold students' writing. The second was much less structured and gave open-ended instructions as to the content and structure of the documentary. Both writing frames contained a 'word bank', with words listed in alphabetical order. These were also differentiated. The words in each bank varied depending on the level of difficulty, allowing the level of sophistication in the vocabulary to be split, as well as the nature of the prompts that students would need. The intention here was to support and guide the use of specific vocabulary for students with different needs. The management of which student was given which writing frame, was planned before the lesson, in respect of formative and summative assessments previously performed. As the class was used to such differentiation there was no protest about which one they received. Figure 5.4 shows the more straightforward writing frame and Figure 5.5 the more difficult one.

These frames were produced to stimulate interest, but also to cater for the needs of different students. They provided a structure that did not provide an answer. Rather it helped to guide and scaffold the production of a piece of written work, leaving many of the important decisions in the hands of each student. Although it was not attempted in this particular example, a very important and fruitful use of writing frames as an extension is to get students to write their own before they begin writing.

This written work took about four hours and two homeworks to complete. The purpose of the drafting process was to allow the writing of the report to be a learning experience in itself. The students were writing to learn and so needed to be given the space in which to make mistakes, revisions and to take risks. Moreover, doing it in this way divorced the skills of thinking from the process of presentation, which helped to monitor and avoid the copying of material. The work was marked before being written up as a final product. However, it was not only the teacher who performed this. Before a member of staff would mark the work, the writers had to have read it themselves, and a friend or partner also had to have read it. Different coloured pen marks were the key to identifying this. This was an important stance to maintain. First, it displaced the teacher as the 'only expert' in the room. It also broadened the audience of the written work beyond adults. Furthermore, it provided another learning experience, and importantly made the marking of the work more manageable.

Bangladesh Flood 1998.

Why did the flood of 1998 have such a big effect in Bangladesh?

Task:
Your task is to produce a photostory which answers the above question using the photographs that you have been given. You will use the photos as the different screenshots, and will then write the words that the narrator would say over the top to tell the story.

You will need to give some background as to where Bangladesh is, and to explain what the causes and effects of the flooding were. After that you must then answer the above question using all the information at your fingertips to come to your own conclusion. You must use at least five of the photographs to tell your story, and must think carefully about what is in your picture and what you are writing for the narrator to say.

Writing Frame:

Introduction:
Bangladesh is located . . .

The landscape of Bangladesh is . . .

In 1998 Bangladesh . . .

Causes of the Flood:
One cause of the flooding was . . .

This meant that . . .

The floods happened . . . .

Dhaka was flooded . . .

A further cause of the flooding was . . .

Effects of the Flood:
One effect of the flooding was . . . .

This meant that . . .

Another effect was . . .

This meant that . . .

Another group of people affected by the flood were. . .

Some people were affected more than others . . .

Conclusion:
So in conclusion, the floods of 1998 had a big effect in Bangladesh because . . .

This happened because . . .

Word bank:

bare	disease	housing	sewage
because	family	livelihood	soil
deforestation	food	poverty	water
delta	health	run-off	which meant
diarrhoea	homeless	savings	work

Figure 5.4   The more supportive writing frame

Bangladesh Flood 1998.

Why did the flood of 1998 have such a big effect in Bangladesh?

Task:
Your task is to produce a photostory which answers the above question using the photographs that you have been given. You will use the photos as the different screenshots, and will then write the words that the narrator would say over the top to tell the story.

You will need to give some background as to where Bangladesh is, and to explain what the causes and effects of the flooding were. After that you must then answer the above question using all the information at your fingertips to come to your own conclusion. You must use at least five of the photographs to tell your story, and must think carefully about what is in your picture and what you are writing for the narrator to say.

Writing Frame:

Introduction:
In this section you will need to introduce where you are going to write about and some clues as to what has happened there. So you will need to explain where Bangladesh and some factual data about the flood that happened in 1998.

Causes of the Flood:
You will now need to explain how the flood was caused. In your writing you will need to group different causes together, such as weather, human activity, landscape of Bangladesh. To produce an excellent piece of geography in this section you need to draw links between these different causes to explain how one cause affected another cause, which may have led to something else happening.

Effects of the Flood:
Having explained how the flood was caused you now need to cover the reasons that it had such a big effect in Bangladesh by looking at the effects that it had. You will need to look at things like disease, health and homelessness as well as a range of other effects. You need to think carefully about how the fact that Bangladesh is a poorer nation changes the effect that the flood had.

Conclusion:
In your final section you need to draw together all of your ideas to answer the question at the top of the page and explain your findings. You will have to try and consider how the fact that Bangladesh is a poorer nation changes the effect that the flood had.

Word bank:

access	diarrhoea	homeless	livelihood	run-off	water
bare	disease	housing	malaria	savings	which meant
because	family	income	poverty	sewage	work
deforestation	food	level of development	risk	snow	
delta	health	links with	resources	soil	

Figure 5.5   The more open writing frame

The finished product

Figures 5.7, 5.8 and 5.9 show extracts from three responses the students produced. They are reproduced here in a specific order which reflects the progression and spectrum of performance in the work that the students created. In Figure 5.6 a summary of the various levels of progression is included, which also points towards the overlap between the Geography National Curriculum and progression in literacy skills.

Level A: A Basic Descriptive Response (at about Levels 3 or 4 of the National Curriculum)
The written response consists largely of descriptive statements, some of which may be straight 'lift-offs' from the cards. The text will be predominantly narrative about the different events that took place in the flood, with little attempt to link, categorise or generalise different elements of the material. For example, there may be no distinction between the human and natural dimensions to the flood. There may also be some error and misunderstanding evident at this level.

Level B: A Semi-explanatory Account (between Levels 5 and 6 of the National Curriculum)
The significant progress that is made into this level is the level of explanation and reasoning contained within the account and the use of categories to make sense of the material. There will be use of detailed material to illustrate the sequence and causes of the flood. This will mean that the written response will contain explanations which develop some links between different groups of factors such as human and natural, or local and national. This differentiation will also be applied to the impacts of the flood to some degree. Within the written text the student will begin to use a range of subject specific vocabulary to convey their ideas as well as prompts such as 'has meant that', 'which means that' and 'another reasons is that'. Students may also begin to prioritise events that caused or happened as a result of the flood. There may still be some error and misunderstanding, but it will be less frequent and serious.

Level C: A Full Explanatory Account (at and beyond Level 7 of the National Curriculum)
At the most sophisticated level the pupils' answers become more detailed and coherent as an analytical structure is applied to the written response in order to develop generalisations about the causes and impacts of the flood. Links are clearly developed between different categories of information, and inferences are made where the student goes beyond the material on the cards. There will be some ranking and prioritising where the student has begun to isolate particular contributory factors and in some cases will relate this to the level of development in Bangladesh. Errors and misunderstanding are far less common at this level of response. The use of technical and subject-specific vocabulary is consistent and appropriate.

NB. Depending on the ability of the group it may be useful to draw out the concepts of 'trigger' and 'background' causes for the students in the oral debriefing so as to extend their understanding towards level C.

Figure 5.6 A summary of progression in this topic

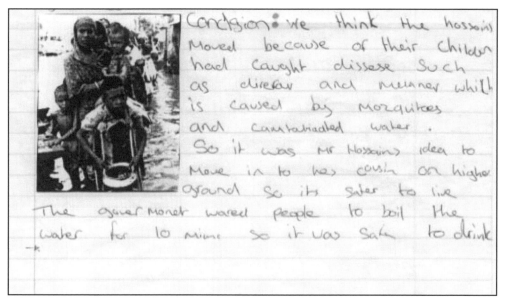

Conclusion: we think the hossins Moved because of their children had caught dissese Such as direrar and meianner whilh is caused by Mozquikes and cantabiadled water. So it was Mr Hossains idea to Move in to hes cousin on higher ground So its Safer to live The gover Monet wared people to boil the water for 10 Minue so it was Safe to drink

Figure 5.7 Colin's conclusion

A student who is at Stage 3 of the SEN register produced the first in Figure 5.7. Colin has a reading age of 7.3 and has a very low concentration span. However, it is clear from his written output here that he has got to grips with some of this content and has produced an answer that attempts to fulfil the brief he was given. The main issue is that he has not drawn generalisations away from the original narrative of the mystery game and is still referring to the two families involved there. He has not bridged his understanding of this to a broader context. He is beginning to make links between the causes and effects of the flood such as the incidence of disease and the issues of contaminated water and mosquitoes breeding. What is totally lacking from this work is any attempt to prioritise or categorise the causes and effects in order to explain the impact of the flood. The spelling errors also undermine the flow of the writing, demonstrating the need to reinforce the use of the word bank and word box activities as teaching activities before the write up. In that his work is descriptive of the process of flooding, this work as a whole represents a basic response to the question.

The next example (Figure 5.8) is from a student named Kyle who has learning difficulties and is also at Stage 3 of the SEN register. Kyle is a student whose oral understanding and communication is far above his written output; he has a reading age of 12.0 and yet a spelling age of 7.9. In fact, he finds writing an inherently painful and threatening process. Given this context there are several key features to note in his work. First, Kyle has produced a significant piece of written work, although it does not truly fit the brief that he was given. However, Kyle composed this largely without the use of a writing frame. This was his decision, which he justified by saying

THE FLOODS IN BANGLADESH 1998

The landscape of Bangladesh has Been distroyed by the 1998 floods wich are proberly the worst the country has sufered in 10 years. One of the main reasons of this is melted snow from the Himalayas wich causes the rivers wich go through Bangladesh to burst their banks which destroyed millions of Homes. There were diseases that followed the floods like milarya and diarya which killed over eight hundred people and left thousands sick and criticly ill.

Finally, I believe the disaster would not have been as bad if the woodland had not been distroed and if people had stopped building around the river banks. The flood would have been a lot less devastating and the loss of life would have been a lot less. This is because cutting the trees and building trees lets more water into the river, The water can't soak into the ground in towns and the trees are not here to soak up the water. People have changed the landscape so the flood was worse.

By Kyle R

Figure 5.8 Kyle's completed piece of work

that the writing frame would come between him and what he wanted to say. The whole piece is somewhat narrative in format, with him almost 'telling the story' of why the floods had such a big effect. This is why it was written as one paragraph, until this was changed when the teacher marked the work in draft. Yet despite the lack of an analytical structure he is clearly attempting to generalise around this central issue, using phrases such as 'The flood would have been a lot less devastating . . .' and 'One of the main reasons of this is . . .'. Kyle is not only attempting to answer the question by explaining both causes and effects, he is making moves towards prioritising and categorising the different parts of the material. His answer links both the human and natural causes of the flood and comes to a clear conclusion with the phrase 'People have changed the landscape so the flood was worse.' Kyle has clearly developed a detailed knowledge of the flood that took place and this is reflected in his use of subject-specific vocabulary. He has begun to explain its causes and effects, and has moved to consider the broader implications of this. The very fact that Kyle produced any written work at all is based on the fact that he was given the opportunity to think and work out his ideas through speech, before he undertook the written task. Writing up his finding was always going to be inherently frightening for him. This work reflects a more sophisticated response as Kyle has explained the process of flooding but has only really just begun to touch upon how it is caused by factors operating at different scales.

An able student, who writes fluently and with independence and flair, produced the final example in Figure 5.9. This student is female, although the divide between the three students here in terms of attainment and gender was not reflected in the class; there were both male and female students at all stages across the attainment spectrum. Kristy produced a mammoth piece of work that was seven and a half sides long. The excerpt printed here (Figure 5.9) is from her conclusion. She worked in partnership with a less able student, and they combined very well together, both benefiting from the support and challenge of working with the other. Her work clearly shows that she is categorising both the causes and effects of the flood, and has linked a wide range of factors into this explanation. Moreover, she has moved beyond the content that was on the cards to consider how the level of development affects the country, and prioritises what she believes to be the most significant cause of the huge impact that the flood had. She has transferred her knowledge from the narrative mystery game to another broader context and has speculated about the possible causes that lie beyond the material on the cards. She uses a range of subject-specific vocabulary that reinforces the authenticity of her 'documentary'. As she is analysing interrelationships between human and natural factors, and processes that operate at different scales, this is definitely a highly advanced and sophisticated response to the question.

It is striking that in all three of these examples, the students have not simply copied information from the texts that they were using. The structure and format of the lessons has meant that each student has been actively involved in manipulating and digesting the material so that they incorporate it into their current understanding. The planned literacy components have clearly allowed access to the curriculum for all students, and have developed their writing, reading and speaking skills.

Making sense of it all

It is impossible to deliver effective lessons without taking into account the role of language as a key element in the learning process. The work that has been outlined here demonstrates how the development of literacy is a central part of the curriculum

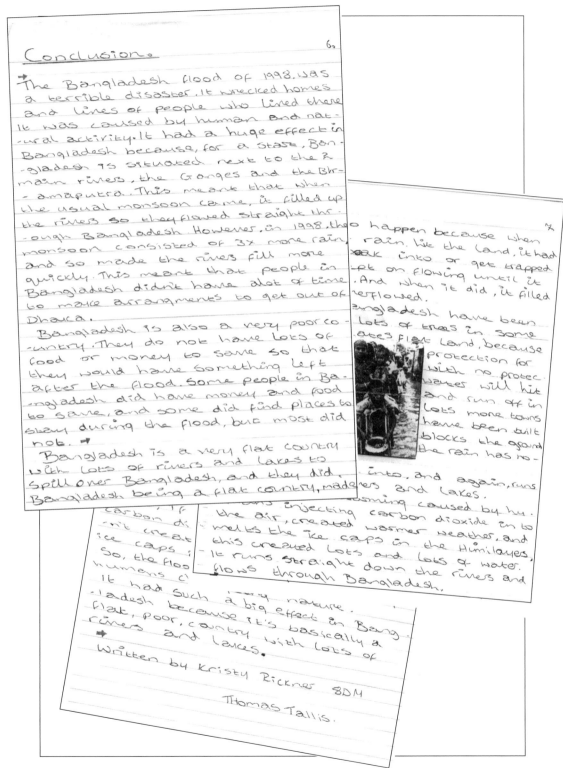

Conclusion.
6.

→ The Bangladesh flood of 1998.was a terrible disaster. It wrecked homes and lines of people who lived there. It was caused by human and natural activity. It had a huge effect in Bangladesh because, for a state, Bangladesh is situated next to the 2 main rivers, the Gonges and the Bhramaputra. This meant that when the usual monsoon came, it filled up the rivers so they flowed straight through Bangladesh. However, in 1998, the monsoon consisted of 3x more rain and so made the rivers fill more quickly. This meant that people in Bangladesh didn't have alot of time to make arrangments to get out of Dhaca.

Bangladesh is also a very poor country. They do not have lots of food or money to save so that they would have something left after the flood. Some people in Bangladesh did have money and food to save, and some did find places to stay during the flood, but most did not. →

Bangladesh is a very flat country with lots of rivers and lakes to spill over Bangladesh, and they did. Bangladesh being a flat country, made ...

... happen because when ... rain, like the land, it had ... into or get trapped ... on flowing until it ... And when it did, it filled ... erflowed.

...angladesh have been ... lots of trees in some ... ...ates flat land, because ... protection for ... with no protec... ...ter will hit ... and run off in ... lots more towns ... have been built ... blocks the ground ... the rain has ro...

... into, and again, runs ...ers and lakes. ... ...ing caused by hu... the air, created carbon dioxide into melts the ice caps in the Himilayes. this created lots and lots of water. It runs straight down the rivers and flows through Bangladesh.

... carbon di... ... creat... ice caps ... so, the floo... humans c...

It had such ... ...ny nature. ... ...ladesh because it's basically a flat, poor, country with lots of rivers and lakes.

→ Written by Kristy Rickner 8DM

Thomas Tallis.

Figure 5.9 An excerpt from Kristy's Conclusion

in all subjects. Moreover, it shows that teaching resources need to be developed, and lessons need to be structured so that the use and development of literacy is planned for and not simply presumed. It is also clear from the work produced here that such an approach facilitates improved performance and understanding in the discrete subject area that is being taught. From this study there are several key areas to draw out in order to make sense of the materials that have been outlined:

- *Asking questions:* the use of key questions to structure the learning process, means that the content is oriented to stimulate investigation and enquiry by the students. Their learning becomes focused on 'finding out', handling data and explaining answers. This also stimulates a sense of wonder in the students, which improves their motivation as it involves them in the work more directly. It also raises issues in the subject matter that contain conflict and different views, that adds a touch of real life to the study, as well as making the learning experience richer and more challenging.

- *Incorporating literacy:* these resources and lessons planned the use of literacy skills directly, and also planned for their development. This meant that the language and information handling skills of the children were not presumed, but rather supported and stimulated during the learning process. By beginning with their previous knowledge and understanding, and then demanding that they actively manipulate the material and texts in front of them, the students were directly involved in the generation of new understanding. The tasks and resources structured the careful use of listening, speaking, reading, re-reading, categorising and writing. Clear objectives and uses of each of these elements of literacy were set, and through the debriefing sessions the students reflected on how they had used and developed these skills. Such an approach should allow the development of these skills to be longer lasting and transferable.

- *Oral work as a central pillar:* through the paired or group discussion in these activities, children are given the forum in which to 'work out' and generate meaning. As Vygotsky has demonstrated, through the very act of speaking, people can crystallise and develop their thinking, and thus any new knowledge and understanding becomes more embedded as part of their own knowledge structures. The use of oral discussion made in these activities enables the pupils to actively manipulate and re-work the material so that they are directly involved in the learning process. Importantly, keeping this as a central pillar also appeals to different 'senses' that go beyond those most often used in secondary school classrooms. The talking that takes place therefore becomes an active agent in the learning process, rather than a destructive deterrent to effective learning.

- *Teaching is about scaffolding:* the model of teaching demonstrated here is very complex, but is based on the belief that teaching is not simply about the transfer of a body of knowledge. More importantly the teacher is one mechanism through which children are given the structure and pathway in which the subject content becomes a vehicle for other skills. This role as an 'expert facilitator' is one where children's learning is 'scaffolded' rather than 'constructed'. This is clearly demonstrated through the careful use of open-ended questions in the various debriefing sessions that take place, and the use of writing frames differentiated to support students at different levels of ability. The outcomes of learning are in some ways modelled by the teacher, and the students then apply this 'expert' view to their own understanding. The eventual aim under this model is that the students should become equipped to carry out the work and learning for themselves, so that the expert facilitator can withdraw.

• *Metacognition in learning:* defined as 'thinking about thinking', metacognition builds upon the last point. Students not only need to be shown what and how to learn; they also need to reflect upon this process for themselves so that they come to an understanding of how they can carry it out independently. The debriefing elements to the lessons demonstrated here are an excellent mechanism for stimulating this, as well as helping to bridge links between what pupils already know and how this can be expanded and made more elaborate. Added to this, planned incorporation of such methods on a regular and consistent basis, allows for the process to become embedded in the way that children approach learning across a school. This is an issue for the organisation and management of the curriculum at the level of individual departments as well as the whole institution.

• *Different literacies within the curriculum:* the work shown here not only develops a student's global literacy skills, but also their understanding of the particular methods and language of Geography as a discrete subject. This might be called a 'geographical literacy'. The variety of technical vocabulary and the genres of writing that take place within Geography are explicitly developed by an overall focus on literacy. This means that students become more effective geographers as they become familiar with the various ways of thinking in Geography. Based on this it is possible to argue that the development of a whole-school literacy policy where common threads are drawn across subjects, can also become a mechanism for enhancing learning in discrete subject areas. This is an area that the department from which these resources emerged is about to tackle.

The questions that have been raised about standards of literacy have provoked a debate that the teaching profession needs to view as a window of opportunity. In the Geography department featured in this chapter, the resources described formed part of a rolling programme of curriculum development. This is now evolving into the department using meeting time to consider the role Geography has in developing literacy, and finally to produce a literacy policy. The involvement of all staff has been a crucial element of this, as has their increasing commitment to it as the performance and success of students has risen.

As an endnote I would like to finish with a thought for the future. At the end of the lesson in Phase 2 of this work, I asked the class the question 'How has talking to somebody else helped your work today?' Quite genuinely, amongst many diverse answers, and without prompt came the response, 'Well it helped us to make sense of it, sir.' In this simple expression, this student grasps the essence of how this approach to language and learning in particular subjects is a force for change and improvement. As we approach the new millennium, a new slogan of 'life-long learning' is proclaimed. The argument here is that we need to equip our young people with learning that has a longer life, so that they become more active and literate agents in their own growth and development.

Chapter 6

Writing about development

Bob Jones, Diane Swift and Dennis Vickers

Following a recent OFSTED inspection, the staff at Alleynes School at Stone in Staffordshire wanted to focus on teaching and learning strategies for their lower attaining students. For the geography department this involved working with two LEA advisers to plan and teach a unit of work to a group of lower ability Year 10 students. The students in the group were chosen because of the diversity of their needs. Within the class there were 'statemented' students and students with specific reading and writing difficulties. The class also included some quite able students with emotional and behavioural difficulties which had limited their academic progress. All of the students in the group were following the NEAB GCSE Syllabus C. We decided to focus on the development unit and on the following concepts:

- Levels of economic development vary spatially at all scales. Each measure of development has its shortcomings and can give only a partial picture.
- The gap between economically more developed and economically less developed countries is very wide and shows little signs of narrowing.

The study of development can present a challenge to the most able of students and their teachers since it often involves the exploration of values. As Trevor Bennetts (1995) states:

> pupils need to develop understanding of how the goals, assumptions, attitudes and values held by people influence their decisions and actions. They also need opportunities to discuss and reflect on such matters so that they can develop well-informed views of their own.

The ability to review and reflect on issues critically is a key aspect of geography education. To develop this ability students need to be both supported and challenged. It is not an ability that students will automatically develop, or that comes from exposure to more and more content. This idea is expressed in the leaflet 'Global perspectives' in the National Curriculum Guidance for Key Stage 3 Geography:

> the issues raised by development education should be discussed with reference to personal and local contexts, as well as distant and global contexts. How young people feel about themselves and their own locality will reflect on the perceptions they have of others in the world around them.   (Development Education Association 1996)

We aimed to incorporate this guidance into our unit of work. We wanted to ensure that the students understood the term development and that they saw development as a local as well as a global issue, both in this country and elsewhere. We also wanted to challenge the students to be active participants in their world. To achieve these goals we needed to develop students' thinking skills, therefore both the content and the process of the learning were of great importance.

Having decided on the geographical focus of our work, we then consulted with Peter Croft (a Special Needs Adviser with Staffordshire LEA). Peter introduced us to writing frames, developed by a team at Exeter University, the Extending Literacy Project (EXEL). Originally developed to support children's writing for the requirements of the English national curriculum, writing frames are very versatile.

> Writing frames are a strategy which help children use their generic structures of recount, report, procedure, explanation, exposition (arguing a point of view) and discussion until they become familiar enough with these written structures to have assimilated them into their writing repertoire.   (EXEL 1995)

A writing frame consists of a skeleton outline to 'scaffold' children's non-fiction writing. The framework consists of various key words or phrases. Figure 6.1 shows one of the writing frames which we used as part of our project.

> The template of starters, connectives and sentence modifiers which constitute a writing frame gives children a structure within which they can concentrate on communicating what they want to say, rather than getting lost in the form. However, by using the form children become increasingly familiar with it.   (EXEL, 1995)

The EXEL team also offer a teaching model (Figure 6.2). This is a model which we used in the project in order to increase the students' expertise gradually. We felt this process supported the development of students' skills through their geography work. Figure 6.3 shows EXEL's analysis of the support that writing frames give. These ideas complement our philosophy, namely that process is as important as content. We also felt it was important to ensure that the learning was at an appropriate pace.

UK and Kenya – a comparison

Although _____ and _____
are different they are alike in some interesting ways.

For example they both _____
_____

They are also similar in _____
_____

They also have the same _____
_____

Finally they both _____
_____

Figure 6.1 One of the writing frames used in the project

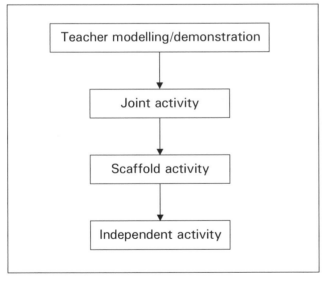

Figure 6.2 The EXEL teaching model

Often, it can be difficult to accommodate all the requirements of a two-year GCSE syllabus into an appropriate teaching and learning programme. Mindful of the fact that we were dealing with low attaining students, we decided to cover a small

Writing frames can help children by:

- Providing experience of a range of generic structures.
- Offering a structure in which the given connectives maintain the cohesive ties of the text, thus helping students to maintain the sense of what they are writing.
- Offering a varied vocabulary of connectives and sentence beginnings, thus extending students' experience beyond the familiar 'and then ...'.
- Encouraging students to give a personal interpretation of the information they have gathered by the careful use of personal pronouns. It is tempting to talk about this process in terms of giving students ownership of the information they are working with.
- Asking students to select and think about what they have learnt by encouraging them to re-order information and demonstrate their understanding rather than just copying out text.
- Enabling students to achieve some success at writing – a vital ingredient in improving self-esteem and motivation.
- Preventing students being presented with a blank sheet of paper – a particularly daunting experience for some students, especially those for whom sustained writing is difficult.
- Giving students an overview of the writing task.

Figure 6.3   The support offered by writing frames

amount of content, in a significant amount of detail. Low attaining students can cope with sophisticated concepts if these concepts are presented to them in an accessible form and if they are given sufficient time to explore the issues. Typically, low attaining students produce unfinished work and have an incomplete understanding of the topics that they have studied. Although the students we were dealing with varied in their learning needs, what they all shared was the characteristic of learning slowly. We therefore planned to devote a significant amount of time to our project, which took place over half a term. Each week the students had two 75-minute periods of geography (Figure 6.4 illustrates our aims while Figure 6.5 shows our teaching plan). The project made use of Key Stage 2 *Nairobi: Kenyan City Life* photopack produced by Action Aid. We wanted the students to develop quite a sophisticated understanding of the concept of development, i.e. that both England and Kenya had areas that were both developed and developing and that development is not only a Third World issue. We prepared a booklet for the students to use in each lesson. This contained the writing frames, and gave the work a progressive structure.

- Make use of a geographical word or phrase that you did not know before.
- Take and record key information from a photograph.
- Talk/write about the key theme of development.
- Describe some differences between a city, country or continent.
- Place Nairobi and Kenya on a map of either Africa or the World.

Figure 6.4   Teaching aims of the project

Figure 6.5 Teaching plan for the Writing frames project

Content questions	Suggested activities	Resources	Notes/evaluation
What are these places like?	Use compass rose to explore Place A (Nairobi, Kenya) and Place B (Stone, Staffordshire). This to be done first individually, then as a class. Summary of class responses on writing frame.	Compass rose (see Note). Photo of Nairobi city centre. Photo of Stone, Staffordshire. Writing frames for photos	This will form the pupils' initial reaction and will be referred to at the end as part of the evaluation.
Where are these places? What information do we have about them?	Find places on map, locate on own world map. Shade map developed/developing areas. Use cards, sort into Kenya, UK and other. Summarise using writing frame.	Atlas, globe, blank world maps, maps of developed, developing countries. Information e.g. GNP, fertility, population about each place written on cards for sorting activity. Writing frame.	Explore where places are, connect known and distant places, make sense of comparisons at country level.
How can we measure rich/poor?	Use car ownership as an indicator for the UK. Use IT program to find out about different levels of car ownership at UK level, county and town level. Summarise information on appropriate writing frame.	Students given partially completed maps. These are to be completed by the students accessing complete information from the computer. Use the information to complete writing frames.	Different stimulus for writing frames. Activity supports students in appreciating that scale makes a difference as to how we view development. There are inequalities at each level, which are often generalised.
What about Nairobi?	Use Action Aid pack to consider different levels of development in Nairobi. Divide class into two unequal parts, smaller 'rich' group, with more photos, larger 'poor' group with few photos. Work in groups to complete writing frames.	Use Nairobi photopack which has images of both rich and poor parts of the city. Divide into two sets. Writing frame to summarise findings. Writing frames to explore the differences between the two groups.	Appreciate variation at local level, giving meaning to the statistics.
What did it feel like?	Explore with the students what it felt like to be in the rich/poor group. What might this experience help you to understand in both Nairobi and Stone?	Writing frame. Summary.	Connect personal, local and distant experiences.
Evaluation	Explore with students: • what they now understand by the term development, and how this may be different from their views at the start of the project; • how they learnt, what they felt about the writing frames, and about the way in which they were asked to work.	Writing frames.	To ensure that students are made aware of not only what they learnt but also how they learnt, so that they can transfer these strategies to new contexts.

Note: The compass rose is an idea developed by the Development Education Centre (Birmingham) as a tool for encouraging students to think about visual material.

To work with lower attaining students, tasks need to be carefully structured. Figures 6.6 and 6.7 show work from one student, and, we hope, demonstrate the structure incorporated into the tasks. Often these students are quite capable of expressing their ideas orally and yet when it comes to transferring ideas to paper they lack confidence. We felt that if the theme was approached in small steps, students would develop a robust understanding of the term development. Our teaching and learning strategies also demonstrated ideas such as interdependence, justice and co-operation.

This was the first time that writing frames had been used by both the teachers and the students involved in the project. Dennis Vickers taught the group, with Diane Swift and Peter Croft team-teaching some sessions. Initially, the students needed support and encouragement to write in sentences. It was suggested to them that the frames were there to give them support so that they could put on paper those thoughts that they often found easier to say than write. The students were also told that although the writing frames may seem repetitive they serve a purpose by allowing the user to concentrate on improving the structure of what they are writing. At this stage their expression of development issues was purely descriptive (Figure 6.7). The students reacted to the stimulus material, and wrote what they saw.

After the third session the standard of writing and geographical reasoning improved for almost all students regardless of their ability. The students became more able to construct coherent sentences, give reasons and explanations, and to make valid use of geographical terms (one of the original teaching objectives).

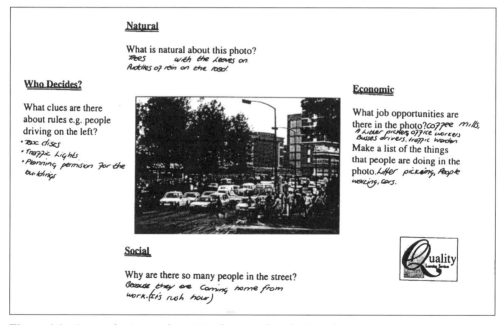

Figure 6.6   One student's use of a writing frame to describe Nairobi city centre

What most surprised me about photo A was

-That people were weaving in and arround the cars whilst they were stopped selling things. The troffic had 3 lanes. There is alot of black men and women. About.

What most surprised the person I spoke to was

• That there was 3 lanes of troffic.
• People were selling things like flowers, clinics, newspapers and food in the troffic.
• Some or most of them were coloured
• The trees are yellow and Green.

They found out the same things as me.
 For example.

• Taxc Oisks
• Litter pickers
• The coffee mill at the back of the picture.
• Puddles on the road.
• It's rush hour.
• Planning permission for buildings

We found out different things.
 For example.

The street lights - rules - when you turn them on or turn them off - what time.

Figure 6.7   One student's description of what they had found out from the photo of Nairobi city centre

As a result of this process, the students began to gain confidence. We found that asking them to read aloud what they had written helped them to recognise the coherence and complexity of their own work. Also, the open nature of the writing frames ensured that they were all able to participate effectively, starting at their own level. The repetition of the structure developed their confidence and enabled the teachers to review the work with the students effectively and meaningfully. This supported the students, helping them to be clear about not only the 'what', but also the 'how' of their learning. They were given a structure from which they could generalise and instead of being swamped with inappropriate content were given time to learn. It was noticeable that students were staying on a task for the full 75 minutes of each session.

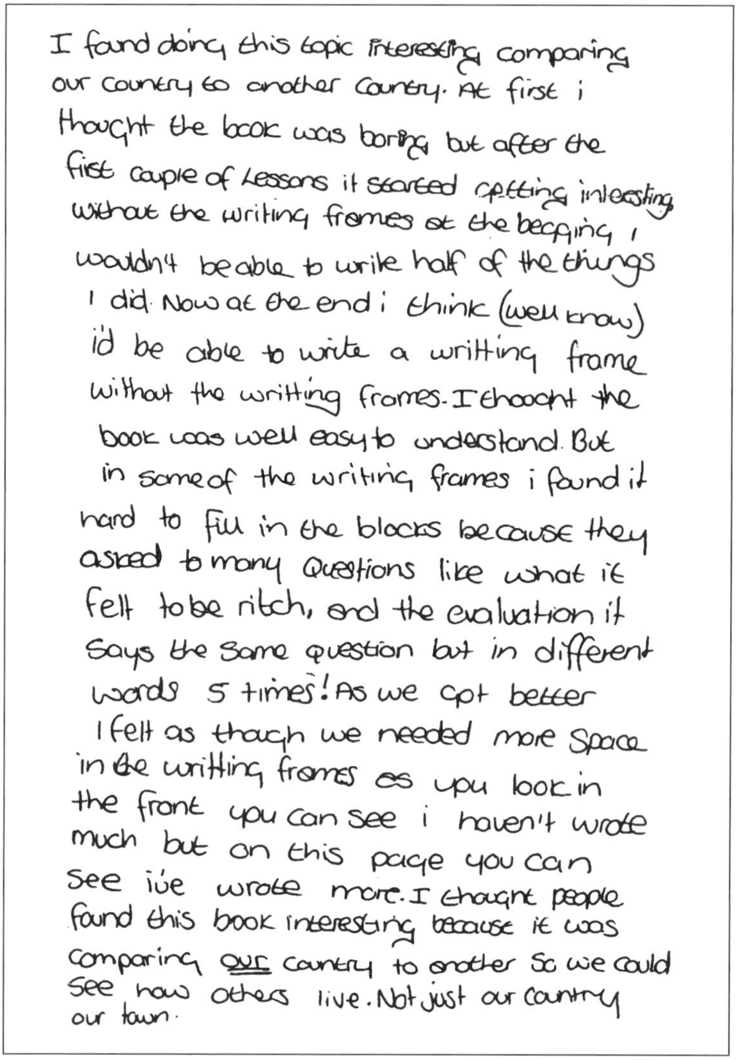

I found doing this topic interesting comparing our country to another country. At first i thought the book was boring but after the first couple of lessons it started getting interesting without the writing frames at the begging, i wouldn't be able to write half of the things I did. Now at the end i think (well know) id be able to write a writting frame without the writting frames. I thought the book was well easy to understand. But in some of the writing frames i found it hard to fill in the blocks because they asked to many questions like what it felt to be ritch, and the evaluation it says the same question but in different words 5 times! As we got better I felt as though we needed more space in the writting frames as you look in the front you can see i haven't wrote much but on this page you can See ive wrote more. I thought people found this book interesting because it was comparing our country to another so we could see how others live. Not just our country our town.

Figure 6.8   One student's evaluation of the writing frames project

After the students had already used the frames for five or six sessions, a couple of them commented that this was repetitive and boring. By the end of the next week the same students were complaining that there was not enough space on the writing frame. Figure 6.8 illustrates a fascinating evaluation made by one of the students, and contains some good advice for us teachers!

Initially, many of the students thought that the booklet was easy, but soon found themselves challenged. The frames supported the students in thinking about priorities. Their work encouraged them to be critical thinkers, to work collaboratively, to explore justice issues, and to consider interdependence. One of the key outcomes of this project was the realisation that it is better to consider a relatively small part of the syllabus in depth than to cover large areas without much support. By doing this we feel that the students gained a high level of understanding of a complex issue, i.e. development.

Postscript

In the term following this project, the students started researching for their GCSE coursework. Having conducted a local survey, the students were asked to analyse and write up their results. As the students were trying to make sense of the information that they had gathered, one was heard to say to the other, 'Lets imagine that we have a writing frame'. It was gratifying to know that the process of learning had been internalised and generalised. Let's hope this lasts!

Acknowledgement

This chapter is reproduced by permission of the Geographical Association. It was first published as an article by Jones, B., Swift, D. and Vickers, D. 'Writing about development', *Teaching Geography* **22**(1), 5–10. Published by the Geographical Association.

Chapter 7

The EXEL Project in a secondary school

Penny Travers

> I have found this EXIT model very helpful in teaching writing in a structured way and would have welcomed working on this while training to be a teacher all those years ago.

> The test results for this module are about 10 per cent higher than usual. Several of the students whose work was monitored closely have done much better than usual.

> One particular student has learning and behaviour difficulties . . . He was so confident in his own work that he felt able to act as a group spokesperson . . . He reported back with confidence and new scientific understanding.

These are some of the comments made by teachers evaluating the impact of working with the EXIT model in their Key Stage 3 classrooms. Experimenting with the approach put forward by the model, teachers across four curriculum areas, Science, Technology, Humanities and English, found particular strategies to be of great benefit to pupils, enabling them to draw on their existing knowledge, to engage with texts and to process and communicate learning. The model supported teachers in planning lessons that allowed pupils to access new and demanding material and to restructure information in order to demonstrate understanding.

In this North London comprehensive school a particular challenge for many of the teachers was to find ways of actively involving all pupils in lessons, including those new to the country and new to English. The school population has changed quite radically over the past five years and currently approximately 40 per cent of pupils are bilingual, of whom a significant number are at an early stage of acquiring English. Over 40 languages are now spoken in the school, Turkish and Somali being the main minority languages. There are increasing numbers of refugees. There is a school focus on developing literacy both for the students who arrive at transfer working towards National Curriculum Level 4 in English and for those more confident and fluent readers and writers. Any materials produced by teachers need to be both accessible and demanding.

All staff in the school attended in-service training to learn about the background to the EXEL project and research, and to begin to consider incorporating the EXIT model in their own planning and teaching. Those teachers who chose to explore implementing the model in some detail worked in partnership with teachers from the borough Language and Curriculum Access Service (LcaS) to develop an inclusive approach to supporting bilingual pupils. Partnership teaching assumes that all pupils are engaged in the learning tasks of mainstream classrooms. It promotes a dynamic approach to curriculum planning and delivery – achieved by mainstream and support staff working closely together and sharing expertise. The teachers involved in this project met regularly to follow the partnership cycle of Review, Set goals, Experiment, Evaluate and Disseminate.

They started by reviewing resources and strategies already in place and identified areas in need of re-working and improving. Next they planned approaches and activities and designed new materials, experimenting in the classroom through shared delivery. They then evaluated the outcomes and disseminated the work developed to other colleagues in their curriculum area and across the whole school. An important aspect of the implementation of the project was the fact that teachers were working collaboratively, thus providing opportunities for sharing and exploring aims and strategies. This approach also emphasised the value of talk as a way of clarifying and developing ideas – something that the teachers focused on in their work with pupils. The EXIT model provided a focus and framework for planning in partnership and also meshed perfectly with the Learning Environment approach – the structured conditions for effective teaching and learning in multilingual classrooms – promoted by LcaS. (See *Making progress in Humanities: scaffolding learning in the multilingual classroom*, LcaS 1997, for a complete account of this.)

The way in which the Learning Environment is understood and organised has a powerful impact on all pupils and particularly on those for whom English is a second or additional language. It informs the way in which they view themselves as learners, how they build on what they know, how they interact and consider information together and how they demonstrate understanding. The central component of the Learning Environment is curriculum planning and delivery and the EXIT model offers a highly effective means of scaffolding learning to allow all pupils to access lesson content and make progress.

Humanities teachers found the initial stages of the model offering 'ways into' new topics to be particularly helpful. In introducing a GCSE module 'People and Place: inequalities in urban areas', they set up collaborative group work and pupils asked questions about cities depicted in a series of photographs. Pupils were then encouraged to group their questions under particular headings and in this way to develop a concept map of the features noted. Pupil reflection on the learning process was overheard during one of the lessons. In reply to the question 'What are we learning from this?', a boy informed his fellow group member, 'You are learning how to ask questions.'

All pupils are supported by visual stimulus and by opportunities to think aloud, to question, challenge, negotiate and listen. Bilingual pupils in particular benefit from the chance to hear ideas being expressed and re-worked and to develop linguistic skills in the context of purposeful tasks.

Teachers in the Science department found that concept maps produced both before and after work on a topic provided a useful means of assessing at a glance the way in which pupils' knowledge and understanding had been extended (Figure 7.1).

Science teachers in this project also focused on using visual material to support interaction with text, encouraging pupils to 'read' actively pictures, photos and diagrams alongside the written word. They made extensive use too of grids and charts as a means of prompting pupils to elicit particular points of information. They went on to make explicit the approaches used to promote literacy development in their schemes of work. The key skills column in their planning grid highlights the EXIT strategies now incorporated (Fig. 7.2).

Following a review of the quality of Year 9 assignments, the Head of Technology was keen to support pupils in writing design briefs. He noted that existing submissions ranged from those negotiated with the teacher who acted as scribe, to those which lacked concise structure or wording or were poorly presented. He became aware of the fact that there was little in place to ensure that pupils progressed to the standard of independent work required for GCSE, noting: 'There may have been an element of "the English department teaches them how to write" leading to an expectation that students would be able to write a brief unsupported.' Working in partnership, he structured a unit on 'Writing a design brief for an alarm' making extensive use of modelling and frames for planning and writing to ensure a succinct and well-presented quality outcome from the students.

In order to monitor pupils' understanding of food safety and hygiene issues, Food Technology teachers produced key words and definitions cards. These could be used in a variety of collaborative activities and revision exercises (Fig. 7.3).

The EXIT model has been used extensively to develop pupils' interactions with non-fiction texts but the process stages lend themselves equally well to fiction and narrative writing. As part of this cross-curricular project, a teacher in the English department worked with a language support teacher to explore the application of the model to pre-twentieth century poetry and the teaching of Tennyson's 'The Lady of Shalott' to a Year 8 class. The class was a mixed ability group of 28 students, 12 of whom were Turkish speakers and three of these pupils were refugees at the initial stage of learning English.

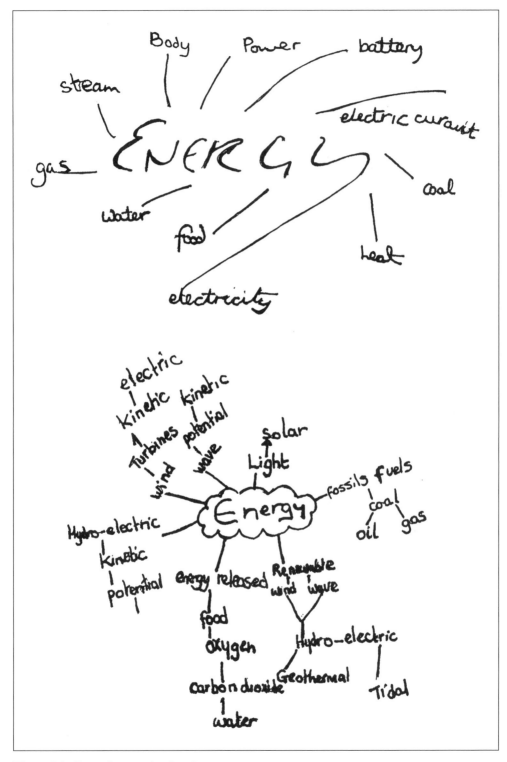

Figure 7.1   Pre and post unit of work concept maps

Figure 7.2 Part of the planning documents for the unit on Energy

Lesson no.	Key skills	Purpose (AT, levels)	Plan (core and extension)	Homework	Safety
1 w/s 1 OHP 1a OHP1b	Literacy Brainstorm Discussion Concept mapping	Sc4 5a There is a variety of energy resources	Ask students to brainstorm the term 'energy'. Display the arising key words on the OHP. Students choose 12 words and work in groups to create a concept map. Discuss the different forms of energy and the Joule as the unit of energy. Introduce w/s 1 for homework. Students match key words to definition/picture	Complete w/s 1	Electrical precautions with the OHP
2 w/s 2a w/s 2b	Discussion Literacy (recording grid) Observing	Sc4 5c Electricity is generated using a variety of energy resources. 5f Energy can be transferred and stored.	Discuss what happens in an energy transfer, SS7 page 34. Students rotate around the energy circus, discussing the transfers that take place. Stress safety considerations before students commence the circus. Students answer questions 1c and 1d on page 37. Discuss responses. Students complete w/s 2a. Explain the homework w/s 2b to students	Complete w/s 2b	Electrical precautions. Beware of cuts. Beware of burns. Beware of dropping heavy objects
3 OHP 3a OHP 3b	Discussion Literacy (text underlining) Drawing energy transfers	Sc4 5f Energy can be transferred and stored. 5g Energy is conserved. 5h Energy can be dissipated	Ask 'Can energy be cretaed/destroyed?' Discuss responses. Students make notes from OHP3a. Discuss examples of energy transfer devices, OHP 3b. Students then answer question 4 on page 35 and question 2 on page 35 of SS7. Introduce the homework	Draw 10 energy transfers of everyday devices found in the kitchen	Electrical precautions with the OHP
4 Generic help sheets	Planning Predicting Discussing Literacy (writing frame) Numeracy Data handling	Sc1 1a–f Planning. 2a–e Evidence. Sc4 5f Energy can be transferred and stored. 5h Energy is dissipated	Introduce the clockwork toy investigation, page 37 of SS7. Discuss how the *distance travelled* by the toy depends on how *many times it is wound up*. Demonstrate the toy. Stress that the toy should not be overwound. Students work in groups to plan and to begin to carry out the investigation. Stress to students that their predictions should include science words	Complete the planning and investigation	Beware of cuts. Beware of dropping objects.

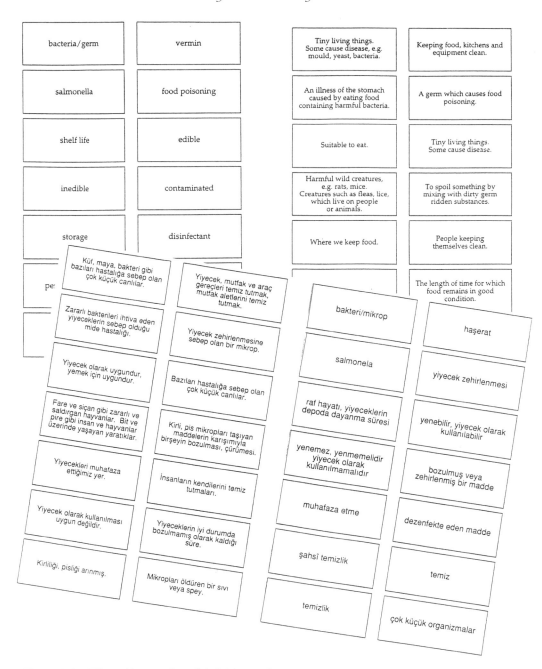

Figure 7.3 Bilingual key words and definition cards

Our aim as teachers was to ensure that we met the National Curriculum requirement that pupils study pre-twentieth century poetry, building on their knowledge of a variety of literature and developing appreciation of 'the distinctive quality' of particular works. The outcomes that we planned for were pupil involvement in making sense of the text – subject, themes and structure – and developing a personal response to the poem.

The unit of work drew on visual and information texts as well as focusing closely on the poem itself and a range of EXIT strategies were used. Pupils began by working in groups to look closely at an illustration from *The Arthurian Tradition* and to write statements and questions about their observations. This activity served two purposes: it activated pupils' prior knowledge about this period and literary genre and it invited them to become enquiring researchers as they moved into reading tasks (Figure 7.4).

Pupils then went on to read the text which accompanies the illustration in the book and to note, in a text marking activity, key points about the history and features of myth and legend. They were then asked to group examples of the key themes under headings provided on a concept map. Some of these concepts became important points of reference during the later readings of Tennyson's poem 'The Lady of Shalott'.

Once familiar with the context of the tale told by Tennyson, pupils started to explore the poem itself, first through sequencing a set of pictures and predicting the story line and then by a close study of the text itself. Again, text marking activities, focusing on different aspects of each of the four parts of the poem, proved to be a very effective means of enabling pupils to read interactively.

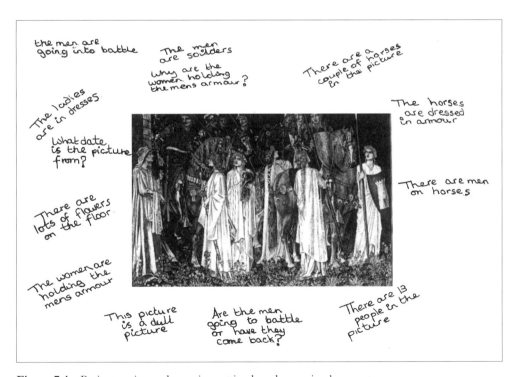

Figure 7.4   Brainstorming and question setting based on a visual prompt

In the exercise shown, pupils worked in pairs to select and underline details of the setting in the poem. They then drew their own illustrations, capturing the mood and detail of the description found in the text. In this way they were supported in processing the information and in producing their interpretation of the scene. For bilingual learners who have grasped a sound understanding of a piece of information or a particular concept but who are at an early stage of developing literacy in English, restructuring text as a diagram, map or illustration is an empowering strategy. Such a task is cognitively challenging, requiring close attention to detail in the text, but does not demand extended written evidence of understanding (Figure 7.5).

The focus for the text marking activity on Part III of the poem was at word level, pupils highlighting colours, adjectives and images depicting light and brightness, a central theme in the description of Lancelot. They used this work in pairs to prepare an oral presentation to the rest of the class, making use of bilingual dictionaries and reading the poem aloud with one of the pupils 'echoing' the highlighted words for dramatic effect.

Having studied the written text in some detail alongside viewing a video of the reading of the poem which makes highly effective use of Charles Keeping's illustrations, pupils worked on a variety of written tasks including a diary entry (Figure 7.6), a newspaper article and narrative writing – a story to make sense of the curse originally placed on the lady. They also examined the structure of the poem. Their final assessment was to write 'the missing verse', one which Tennyson might have included had he allowed the Lady of Shalott to cry out to Lancelot, capturing the appropriate form, tone and language. The writing frame here (Figure 7.7) consists only of the required number of beats or syllables in each line and the refrain. The teachers modelled the process with the whole class, inviting contributions from pupils and noting these on the board for discussion and development. Pupils then worked in pairs to create their own verses, drawing on their understanding and appreciation of the original poem as well as allowing themselves a certain empathic free rein! (Figure 7.8.)

All teachers involved in the project gave feedback on the way in which using the EXIT model had made an impact on their approach to teaching and on the pupils' learning. They expressed enthusiasm for 'strategies that really work', new methods of involving pupils actively in tasks and of consolidating learning. They noted enhanced pupil motivation, confidence and sense of satisfaction: 'They seemed proud to show what they had learnt.' They made suggestions too for the way in which the school could extend the approach, including increased sharing of good practice across subject areas and development of whole-school policy. As literacy development increasingly becomes a focus for secondary schools and consideration is given to the way in which continuity and progression across the phases is ensured, the EXIT model offers a very real way forward.

Picturing the setting

Circle words or phrases
that refer to the landscape

> On either side the river lie
> Long- fields of barley and of rye,
> That clothe the wold and meet the sky;
> And thro' the field the road runs by
>   To many tower'd Camelot;
> And up and down the people go,
> Gazing where the lilies blow
> Round an island there below,
>   The island of Shalott.

Draw a box round words
or phrases that describe
buildings.

> Willows whiten, aspens quiver,
> Little breezes dusk and shiver
> Thro' the wave that runs forever
> By the island in the river
>   Flowing down to Camelot.
> Four gray walls and four gray towers,
> Overlook a space of flowers,
> And the silent isle imbowers
>   The Lady of Shalott.

Underline the names
of plants.

> By the margin, willow-veiled.
> Slide the heavy barges trail'd
> By slow horses: and unhailed
> The shallop flitteth silken-sail'd,
>   Skimming down to Camelot:
> But \who hath seen her wave her hand?
> Or at the casement seen her stand?
> Or is she known in all the land.
>   The Lady of Shalott?

Put a wavy line
underneath words or
phases that mention
people or animals.

> Only reapers, reaping early
> In among the bearded barley,
> Hear a song that echoes cheerly
> From the river winding clearly.
>   Down to tower'd Camelot:
> And by the moon the reapers weary.
> Piling sheaves in uplands airy,
> Listening, whispers " Tis the fairy
>   Lady of Shalott."

Write a list here of words that are new to you and look them up in a dictionary.

wold   imbowers   aspeh   casement
Sheaves   shallop   flitteth

Now draw your own picture of the setting for this poem based on the information in
the verses.

Figure 7.5   Text marking the poem prior to drawing the setting

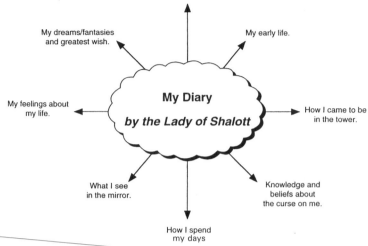

My real name and background.

My dreams/fantasies and greatest wish.

My early life.

My feelings about my life.

My Diary

by the Lady of Shalott

How I came to be in the tower.

What I see in the mirror.

Knowledge and beliefs about the curse on me.

How I spend my days

Dear Diary,

I need to pour out my thoughts and feelings onto paper.

My days are spent . . .

and I feel

I find myself thinking about

When I look in the mirror I see

Sometimes I fantasise that

When I think back to my childhood I r emember

Then a terrible curse was put on me. All I know about it is

I wish

Figure 7.6 Student planning prompt and writing frame for diary entry

The Lady of Shalott – The Missing Verse

Look closely at this verse, the last one in Part III, describing what happens after the Lady of Shalott caught sight of Lancelot in the mirror.

> **She left the web, she left the loom,**
> **She made three paces thro' the room,**
> **She saw the water-lily bloom,**
> > **She look'd down to Camelot.**
> **Out flew the web and floated wide;**
> **The mirror crack'd from side to side;**
> **"The curse is come upon me!" cried**
> > **The Lady of Shalott.**

- How many lines are there?   _____

- How many beats in each line?   _____

- Which words and phrases are repeated? _____

- Using different colours, show the rhyme scheme – underline all the words that rhyme in one colour.

- Now imagine what Tennyson might have written if he had included one more verse here – the verse in which the Lady of Shalott cries out to Lancelot and asks for help, expresses her feelings or gives an opinion. You might start with one of these lines:

"Oh gallant knight so fair of face . . ."
"Dear Lancelot, now stay awhile!"
"The curse is come, oh woe is me!"

- Use the frame below to help you. Each space is one beat.

    ___   ___   ___   ___   ___   ___   ___   ___
    ___   ___   ___   ___   ___   ___   ___   ___
    ___   ___   ___   ___   ___   ___   ___   ___
    ___   ___   ___   ___   ___   ___   ___   ___
    ___   ___   ___   ___   ___   Camelot.
    ___   ___   ___   ___   ___   ___   ___   ___
    ___   ___   ___   ___   ___   ___   ___   ___
    ___   ___   ___   ___   ___   ___   ___   ___
                    The Lady of Shalott.

Figure 7.7   Create the 'missing' verse

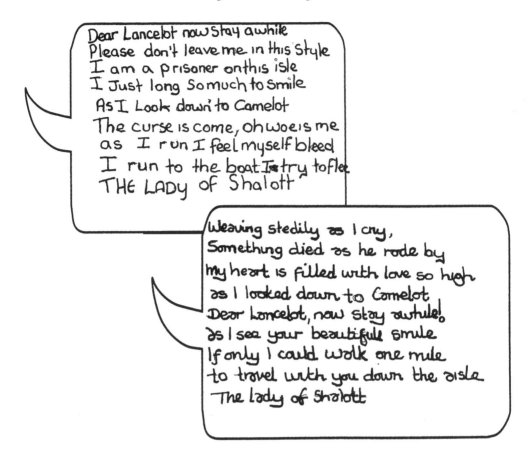

Figure 7.8 Example of students' 'missing' verses

Postscript

The approaches and materials discussed in this account were developed in partnership by Claire Adamson, Sarah Cave, Anne Dobson, Catharine Driver, Rosemary Ellison, Alison Heap, Terry Humphries, Darren Luckhurst, Maggie Scott, Paul Spychal and Penny Travers at Lea Valley High School, inspired and supported by Maureen Lewis.

Chapter 8

Introducing guided reading into Year 7 English lessons

Karen Kitt

Plumstead Manor School is an all girls comprehensive with approximately 1,500 pupils (including post-16 students). It is situated on the southwest fringes of the London Borough of Greenwich in an area which has a mixture of large council housing estates and small Victorian terraced housing. The population of the area is largely working class and is ethnically mixed with a large Asian community. The school attracts pupils from 25 primary schools. On entry the reading ages range from six to age appropriate level. The school has a Language Development Department which offers extra support to students with English as an additional language and a Special Needs Department which supports students with literacy or other needs. In English lessons in Year 7–11 the students are taught in mixed ability classes and they have four periods of English a week.

The Key Stage 3 reading lesson: the need for change

At the start of 1998 the English Department were continuing to encourage reading through the established system within the school. Within the Year 7 English lessons students were having a private reading lesson of around 45 minutes for one period a week. Students could bring in their own reading book during these sessions or choose from the class book-box. The choice of books was largely left to the students. The aim of this reading time was to encourage silent, sustained reading as we were conscious that opportunities for extended reading are relatively rare in the secondary school. However, although as an English team we were committed to providing extended reading opportunities and although some students really enjoyed these lessons and were conscientious about bringing in a reading book, we did have some reservations about the effectiveness of the activity. We identified the following inadequacies:

- A significant number of students in each class did not bring their book to lessons and so ended up reading a bit of one text from the book-box one week, then another bit from another text the next week. This random dipping into texts seemed unlikely to encourage students to develop their responses to texts. It also gave the message that finishing a book was not important.
- Some students were clearly not motivated to read privately and silently. They had difficulty in concentrating or engaging with the text. Quite a lot of 'page turning' was going on but we questioned whether they were actually reading or merely going through the motions to keep the teacher at bay.
- Some students chose texts that were not particularly challenging for their level of ability. This represented a missed opportunity for students to develop their reading skills, to extend the range of texts they might read and to engage at an intellectual level with challenging material.
- The teacher had limited opportunities for assessing reading. Even if teachers took the opportunity to 'hear' some pupils read on a one to one basis, such encounters were usually too brief to give any detailed picture of a student's abilities, responses and interests. With classes of 30 students, opportunities to read with the teacher only occurred infrequently.
- There was insufficient dialogue about what the students were reading and how they read. Engaging students in individual conversations about their reading could be an intimidating experience for some students. The individual reading sessions did give some information on the strategies students were using when they encountered problems in their reading but again we felt this was too patchy and infrequent to be of real value. There were few opportunities to explicitly support students in developing a range of reading strategies and to offer positive feedback on their reading.

There were further factors which also prompted us to consider whether it was time to change our existing practices. We had a growing awareness that the literacy hour, just being introduced into the primary school, was increasingly likely to have an impact upon our students. We had run a Summer Literacy School within the school the previous summer and wanted to build upon the reading experiences the Summer Schools offered students; we wanted to work in a more integrated way with our colleagues in the SEN and Language Development departments. We also wanted to update our own knowledge of a range of reading teaching strategies and approaches.

Introducing guided reading

Guided reading and shared reading were terms we had all encountered but our first need was to clarify what each involved and decide whether they would be of help to our students. Within the Framework of the National Literacy Strategy (DfEE 1997a) guided reading is defined as:

> . . . the counterpart to shared reading. The essential difference is that in guided reading . . . the teacher focuses on **independent** reading . . . rather than modelling the processes for pupils.

With the support and advice of Maureen Lewis from the Nuffield EXEL Project we had a series of joint meetings between the English, SEN and Language Development departments in which we tried a guided reading session for ourselves, examined videos of children undertaking guided reading sessions (these were mainly primary children) and began to select books to use with our students. Members of the English Department then further researched and selected the texts and prepared extension materials to go with the sets of books. Examples of the kind of materials we produced are given later in the chapter.

Our first introduction to guided reading was at our own level – using William Boyd's *Blue Afternoon* as our text. We knew that guided reading took place in small groups with each member of the group having their own copy of the same text. The text is selected as being at the reading level of the group with a small area of challenge. The challenge can be in the level of reading difficulty or in the content of the book. The session is lead by a teacher or other adult and has four stages:

- Introduction to the text/reading strategies
- Reading the text
- Discussion of the text/strategies
- Follow up activities.

In a group of about six, all with our own copy of the text, we first considered the front cover without being allowed to look at the back or inside. Our speculations and predictions were questioned and we had to articulate our reasons. Within the group we discussed ideas, one person noticing the small flag, another the hint of ships and colonial buildings and so on. Our joint speculations were richer and more varied than our individual speculation had been – as Vygotsky (1968/1978) tells us, our joint consciousness is greater than our individual consciousness.

Before we opened the book and began reading we were each given a couple of 'post-it' notes and told that if anything occurred to us as we read – questions, responses, unknown words and so on – we were to jot them down. With less experienced readers the teacher would ask the group what they might do if they got stuck (read on to see if it becomes clear, re-read, sound out, use any visual cues and so on). The teacher might also select one or two words that they anticipate will cause difficulties and draw students' attention to these before they beginning reading. When the reading began our group was instructed where to stop and to all read individually in silence. With less experienced readers, students are encouraged to read individually but quietly 'under their breath' so the teacher can listen in. The teacher stays with the group looking out for the strategies she can observe being used, praising when a strategy is used independently by the student and intervening when a student is having difficulties. Guided reading is not 'round robin' reading although 'round robin' reading can also be used to good purpose in group situations like these. Many primary teachers use a combination of different group reading approaches within the literacy hour.

When all the students have read to the agreed spot the group can then discuss what they have read with the teacher questioning for understanding, encouraging responses, getting students to check their predictions and so on. With older and more fluent readers the reading of an agreed portion of the text could be undertaken before the lesson so that the guided session with the teacher can be devoted to 'book talk' (Chambers 1993). In our group, our gender expectations were challenged by reading the prologue and this lead to an interesting and lively discussion. Although we ourselves did not undertake a follow-up activity on this occasion, the use of independent follow-up tasks such as character charts, dictionary work, empathetic writing and so on became an important part of our classroom work with our students.

Having experienced for ourselves the concentrated attention the teacher gives one group during the guided session and the importance of the group not being constantly interrupted, we had to consider what would be happening to the rest of the class when we introduced this way of working into our classrooms. It was decided that during the implementation phase of the 'new' reading we would need to ensure that the reading lesson was timetabled for a session when another member of staff was working in the room. This person, from the Language Support Team, would play a wider role with the rest of the class rather than working on support for a few individuals. This additional adult proved to be vital to the success of the implementation phase, although ultimately as the system becomes established it may be possible to operate with just one teacher in the room.

How does the new reading lesson work?

Implementing the new approach to reading meant rethinking our stance on mixed ability teaching. Whilst still committed to this approach in most of our English sessions, students are grouped for this one English session according to their reading ability. Groups are broadly defined as 'more able', 'middle', 'lower middle' and 'less able'. This works out as five or six students in a group. This grouping allows us to identify books appropriate for each group's differing reading needs. Over time the groups have developed a sense of 'reading identity' within their groups. They can share their thoughts, pleasure or dislike of a book, secure in the knowledge that they will not stand out as the 'thickie' or the 'boffin' within their group.

The teacher has a resource box which contains four short sets of books which are appropriate for each group's reading ability. A folder accompanies each set of books which gives instructions as to how much the students should read and tasks on each section of the text (see Figure 8.1).

The tasks are designed to promote reading skills and enjoyment of the text. They are written so that each group can read the tasks and work independently on them. For example, with the book *Pinballs* by Betsy Byars (used by a lower middle reading ability group), having read Chapters 17 and 18 during guided reading the students are then given an extension activity which asks them to sequence events involving one of the characters and categorise them as either 'ups' or 'downs' (see Figure 8.2).

The English teacher works with one group at a time for the guided reading element. She listens to students read and teaches reading strategies. She questions students about their reading of the text, their responses and reactions to the story. While this is going on, a support teacher from the Language Development Department makes sure that the other groups are on task and working effectively, or works with another group for the guided session. The other groups are continuing to read further sections of their group readers or completing extension tasks.

As the students have this lesson just once a week, it takes a term to read a whole text. The lower ability groups read two shorter texts within this time. From feedback from students, we have learnt that students do not like longer chapters to be broken

---

'Zlata's Diary'

At the start of each reading session, you must read the instructions below. This is very important!

Read the pages you are told to and then do the activities. If you finish early there is a list of other choices at the back of this folder.

Session 1

Look carefully at the front and back cover (including the blurb). What do you think the book might be about?

What is a diary? When do people write diaries and who are they written for?

Now read the introduction to the diary.

What sort of experiences will Zlata write about?

Look at the list of friends and relations. Have a go at pronouncing the names. Break down the names into syllables to help you:

    example: **Rad   mil   a**   (Radmila)

    example: **Bim   bil   im   bi   ca**   (Bimbilimbica)

Test each other on saying the names. See if you can find different ways of pronouncing the same name.

Figure 8.1   An example of a teacher overview sheet for the book *Zlata's diary* (continued)

Session 2

Read entries 2nd September–Wednesday 27th November 1991

What have you learnt about Zlata so far? Draw this chart in your journal. Use a whole page. As you read the book fill it in. You can start by putting in the things you have learnt so far.

Zlata
Her likes and dislikes
Her personality
Her feeling for family/friends
Her reaction to things happening around her

Session 3

Read Friday 29th November 1991–Monday 13th January 1992

Fill in more details on your chart about Zlata.

Session 4

Read Thursday 5th March–Tuesday 21st April

Pick out the words Zlata uses to write about the war. Copy the chart into your journal and put the words into the right column:

Noun (naming word)	Verb (doing word)	Adjective (describing word)
barricade	destroyed	terrible

Figure 8.1 (continued)   An example of a teacher overview sheet for the book *Zlata's diary*

Session 5

Read Wednesday 22nd April–Wednesday 27th May

Look at the words Zlata has written in capital letters at the start of her diary on 27th May.

Choose one of them to use in a headline for a newspaper article about the war in Sarajevo. Include **all** the words somewhere in your report. You will have to re-read bits of the diary to check certain facts.

Session 6

Read Wednesday 10th June–Sunday 5th July

Look at the pictures of Zlata and her family in the middle of the diary. Which picture would you choose to go on the front cover of a new edition of the diary? Explain your choice using the following sentence stems:

> I would choose the picture which shows . . .
>
> Zlata seems . . . in this picture.
>
> It sould be effective on a front cover because . . .
>
> Pictures help the reader to . . .
>
> I would choose colour/black and white pictures because . . .

Session 7

Read Wednesday 29th July–Saturday 19th September

Mum is obviously suffering as well during the war. Think about the things which would upset and disturb her. Write an entry for mum's diary using the facts Zlata has given us.

Session 8

Read Monday 15th March–Sunday 2nd May 1993

Look carefully at the second paragraph of Monday 15th March. Work as a group to turn this paragraph into a poem called 'Sarajevo is Slowly Dying'.

A language technique called personification has been used in this title. Look up this word in a dictionary and then your teacher will check to see if you understand it.

Session 9

Zlata's diary is being published and this is the promotion day!

Read Saturday 17th July–Wednesday 18th August

Imagine you are a journalist from a famous newspaper or TV station who has been asked to interview Zlata. Write a list of questions you would ask her.

Last Session

You might not have time to cover all the entries you have been asked to read. Don't worry! You can read the 'Afterword' on page 187 to find out what happens to Zlata.

Figure 8.1 (continued)   An example of a teacher overview sheet for the book *Zlata's diary*

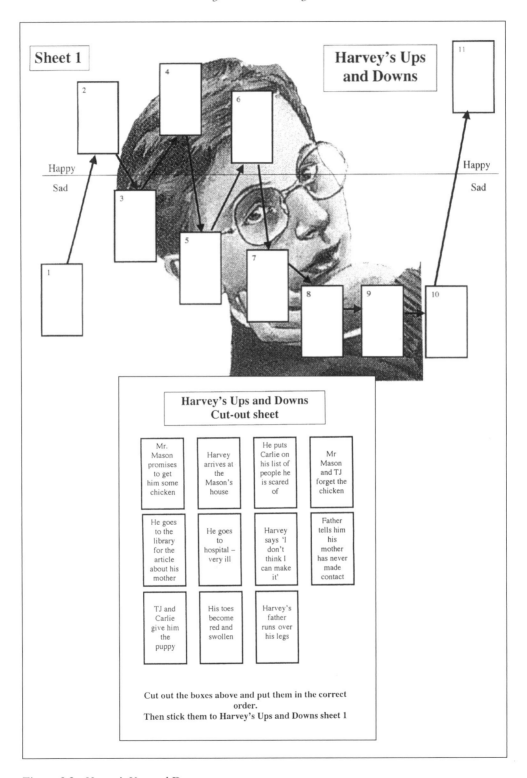

Figure 8.2 Harvey's Ups and Downs

up by activities. It is quite important to achieve a balance between planning activities which encourage students to further their understanding of the text and maintain the momentum of their reading. Students have maintained their enthusiasm for the reading of the text but a few are frustrated by the activities as they interrupt the reading. It is interesting to note however that these students tend to be the more able, independent readers. One advantage of the extended period devoted to a text is that all students do get to read whole novels whereas before many did not have the stamina or inclination to do so.

The success of the new reading lesson

We have been very pleased with the success of our new approach to the reading lesson. Both staff and children are positive about its benefits and we now plan to extend the approach into other year groups. We feel that the more focused guided reading session has the following features to recommend it:

- The experience of reading is more stimulating, active and engaging for students. They enjoy the shared aspect of the reading and help each other stay on task. When asked their views after two terms of the new system students responded with comments such as 'It's fun. It helps you read out loud and build your confidence', 'I prefer reading in a group to on my own. When you're stuck, people can help you.'
- Students talk to each other about what they have read. This building up of a shared ethos where book talk is the norm has an important role in helping students see 'what it is that reading is good for' (Meek 1988). The power of peer pressure is very strong and reading and talking about reading is not a natural part of teen culture for many students. Creating a context in which it is good to talk about books is an important aspect of our new reading sessions: 'You get to communicate and discuss whatever book you're reading. You can argue with each other', 'You learn about each other in the group.'
- Students feel confident and secure in their groupings and are keen to read aloud. They enjoy the teacher's attention and praise when she works with their group. This positive reinforcement is vital in building self-esteem and enthusiasm, especially in struggling readers In the guided reading session students get the teacher's undivided attention for about 30 minutes. This is far more time than could be given to them during an individual one to one reading session.
- The wide range of needs within a mixed ability class is met through differentiated resources and tasks. The students enjoy the follow up activities which both extend and reinforce their understanding of the text, 'It helps me read properly and in detail. I get to understand the characters and plot better.' The students are faced with demanding but achievable tasks according to their needs.

- Strategies for tackling difficult or unfamiliar vocabulary, heeding punctuation, using a dictionary and thesaurus, digging into the text for implied meaning, re-reading to retrieve information, identifying language techniques, etc., can be explicitly taught at the point of need. Teaching in this manner is very powerful. Students can see the relevance of what they are doing. The teaching is contextualised rather than a series of decontextualised skills and the feedback from the teacher is immediate and focused.
- Really informative assessment opportunities are provided. The teacher learns about how individual children read. All of us who have been working in this way feel we know more about our students' reading abilities, reading likes and dislikes, and their responses to a text, that we have ever known before. As one member of staff said, 'I really feel that I know my students as readers. I am far more confident about making assessments in terms of National Curriculum levels for reading.' Such detailed knowledge of our students can inform our planning in other aspects of English and helps us respond to students' individual needs.

Conclusion

Introducing a guided reading session to replace the private reading session demanded a great deal of hard work from staff in order to prepare tasks and resources; to identify suitable books and to create group sets. It also required a budget in order to buy new books, especially those which provide engaging, age suitable content for lower ability readers. These things were possible only with the support and hard work of the three departments involved, the backing of the senior management team who created meeting times for the group and the help of critical friends such as Val Mcgregor (Secondary Literacy Consultant for Greenwich) and Maureen Lewis from EXEL. There is still work to be done as we develop this approach for the whole of Year 7 next year (eight classes) but this hard work seems worthwhile. As a professional English team we feel our thinking and teaching has developed and the reading skills and enthusiasm of our pupils has been enhanced. As a Year 7 student says, 'It's helped me read properly and in detail. I can read more quickly now and understand big words.'

Acknowledgements

The following members of staff all contributed to the development and implementation of the reading session: Amanda Hitchcock, Karen Kitt, Martyn Pendergast, Claire Taeger.

Chapter 9

The LITDOC – a collaborative approach to literacy

Barbara Hersey

South Dartmoor Community College is a forward thinking 11–18 Community College with 1,200 students at present and rising. We are fortunate, in the present educational climate, to be in a position of increasing staffing levels instead of being in the invidious position of losing colleagues. The College is set within the boundaries of the Dartmoor National Park and has a catchment area of over 360 square miles. It has nine main feeder primary schools but our intake increasingly includes about a fifth of students from out of the catchment area.

The College's mission statement is 'Achieving World Skills through participation and performance' and it is to this end that all staff work. Our aim is not only to achieve excellent examination results but to acknowledge that there are students whose achievements are not so easily measured: students who have shown a commitment to learning in spite of particular difficulties. The Learning Support Department is particularly keen that every student realises their potential in whatever way possible and works hard to make this a reality.

The Learning Support Department includes the Special Educational Needs Coordinator (SENCO) and seven learning support assistants who are employed to support students with exceptional arrangements, others considered under detailed arrangements together with all students on the special needs register as described by the national Code of Practice. As a College we have developed expertise in supporting students with an extensive range of difficulties. All members of the team are highly professional and are currently following a Classroom Assistant's Accreditation course which requires written assignments of a high standard. The modules on the course cover literacy, numeracy, emotional and behavioural difficulties and inclusion. Prior to this they have all had the opportunity to develop skills in key areas such as hearing/visual impairment and they now find themselves very skilled. All members of the team have their own expertise to offer and are valued for their contribution. We feel that we have responded to the government's paper *Excellence in*

Schools (DfEE 1997c) which stated that it is only with 'appropriate training' that classroom assistants will be able to make an enhanced contribution to the learning process in schools' (p. 51).

The team realised that they were in a very privileged position within the College as they saw students in a range of subjects areas, across different age ranges and being exposed to different learning and teaching styles. They, more than anyone in the College, had an overview of the learning experiences and difficulties to which students were being exposed. Departments in the school, as in most secondary schools, tended to work in isolation as a result of the nature of the subject material they teach and of the small amount of time available for cross pollination! Learning support assistants, however, were in the unique position of seeing specific skills successfully taught in every department, skills which we felt were easily transferable.

The team meets on a weekly basis during a lunchtime, which in itself shows a commitment to the College. As a result of numerous discussions, some through celebration and some through frustration, we decided that we had something to offer the College particularly in the sharing of ideas. In a recent survey (Dew-Hughes *et al.* 1998) of the training and professional development of learning support assistants, it was found that 'Delegates preferred to see the relationship with teachers as a collaboration, or multiprofessional alliance, where each was fully aware of the skills, gifts and talents you bring to the job.' This gave us confidence in what we were trying to achieve.

Our main concerns

Two areas of concern really hit us. One was that staff would welcome help with setting targets on Individual Education Plans (IEPs). We, as a College, had worked hard at trying to make our IEPs effective, manageable and realistic, but staff still felt slightly threatened when having to set subject specific targets, or indeed any targets. We wanted to help with this process of setting achievable targets and suggesting strategies. We also felt that because of the expertise gained by our learning support assistants, we wanted them to be able to share good practice in an easily accessible way.

The establishment of our aims and objectives was vital. Our aim was to promote literacy through practical suggestions. Our objectives were:

- to promote literacy as the responsibility of all staff;
- to encourage all staff to think about the nature of literacy, that is to create their personal definitions of literacy;
- to identify pupil learning difficulties;
- to offer strategies to help staff overcome those difficulties;
- to share existing good practice;

- to raise achievement by directly addressing literacy problems and achievement;
- to produce support materials which were user friendly with as little reading as possible;
- to assist with the setting of literacy targets on IEPs;
- to encourage dialogue between staff as a way of helping overcome problems.

How to do this?

Our aim was, as already stated, to promote literacy through practical suggestions. We wanted to create a document which would support this aim and could be used by as many staff as possible. With this in mind we initially brainstormed as many difficulties as we could think of which students might experience. These included difficulties such as specific literacy difficulties, recording, spelling, communication skills as well as more defined areas such as dyspraxia and hearing and visual impairment. We were aware that our list was not exclusive but it was a start!

We then took each identified area of student difficulty in turn and brainstormed, from our own experience, and from observed practice, any teaching strategies which we thought would be helpful in remediating that particular problem. We agreed that each classroom assistant would nominate one or two areas of interest to work on further. They took away with them the ideas we had already brainstormed but also agreed to trawl other sources to see if there were other teaching strategies which might be useful. At no time did we expect our ideas to be exclusive or exhaustive! Having collated our ideas we had then to agree on a way of formulating them into a useable document.

What form would the document take?

We wanted our document to be, using the jargon, 'user friendly' and 'a working document'. With this in mind we needed to limit the amount of reading necessary to access the information we were providing. By taking each area of student difficulty in turn, establishing teaching strategies appropriate to that difficulty and cross-referencing these to further sources of information we hoped we had come up with a format.

A means had to be found whereby reading was minimised, but rapid access was assured. The reader had to be directed quickly through the document to find the needed information. A 'Troubleshooting page' was created to assist users of the document to do so with as little difficulty as possible (see Figure 9.1).

Our initial brainstorming had already aligned problems with solutions. Rather than giving the reader a long list of page numbers linked to problems we often directed

Troubleshooting page

Is the problem . . .	see page . . .
communication skills	3
worksheets	4, 5
basic reading	6
reading + (making the most of text)	9
handwriting	16
writing independently	39
spelling – general strategies	20
spelling – specific strategies	21
spelling – subject specific	32
presentation	53
dyslexia	50, 55
dyspraxia	55
disorganised	55
hearing impairment	56
English as an Additional Language	58
visual impairment	59

Meeting IEP literacy targets

Some typical IEP literacy targets:

to develop reading skills	6, 9
to develop independent reading skills	6, 9
to develop writing and spelling skills	16, 20, 21, 32, 39, (53)
to develop literacy skills	check other targets
to develop phonic knowledge	6, 21
to read and write digraphs	6, 21
to read and write 100 words	6, 21, 22
to give key vocabulary for topics	32
to improve spelling	20, 21, 32
to improve oral participation and listening skills	3, (56)
to improve recording skills	9, 16, 39, 53
to extend spelling ability	20, 21, 32
to improve handwriting	16, (20, 21, 32)

Figure 9.1 Troubleshooting page

him or her to spider diagrams which by asking further questions forced a clarification of the problem being encountered and then a choice to be made in response to it (see Figure 9.2). These pages sharpened the focus and then sent the reader to the precise page they needed.

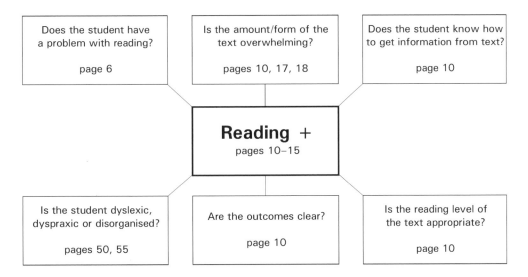

| Does the student have a problem with reading? page 6 | Is the amount/form of the text overwhelming? pages 10, 17, 18 | Does the student know how to get information from text? page 10 |

Reading +
pages 10–15

| Is the student dyslexic, dyspraxic or disorganised? pages 50, 55 | Are the outcomes clear? page 10 | Is the reading level of the text appropriate? page 10 |

Figure 9.2 Spider diagram – reading

We needed staff to know, for example, that if a student had a specific spelling difficulty they could refer to the correct section and access a list of strategies that they could try. Equally, if the student's problem lay in organising ideas prior to independent writing, a list of strategies to meet this need could quickly be found.

To give an example of how this process worked we have included a further three sections from the completed document. The first, shown as Figure 9.3, is a copy of the document page to which readers are directed in the event of the identified student problem being basic reading.

The second example shows firstly (Figure 9.4) the page to which readers would be directed if the student problem they had selected from the Troubleshooting page was handwriting. Having clarified the problem using this spider diagram they would then turn to a further page (Figure 9.5) which contained more detailed information and suggestions.

The process of devising this document took a great deal of time and consultation between members of the team. Fortunately some of the work was undertaken in the Summer term of 1998 when we had some flexibility with time slots made vacant by Year 11. We acknowledge that our time could otherwise have been used to give support to younger pupils during this period, but we decided to make the LITDOC, as we had now decided to call it, our priority. Hopefully staff would appreciate our efforts.

Basic Reader

Is there a problem with vision?
- Check if the student has had a sight test recently. Student may 'miscue' or squint. (Eyesight may change at puberty.)
- Check with student that the print size is appropriate.
- A colour filter is sometimes useful. See SENCO.

Does the student know phonics/blends?
- Test single letters, digraphs (ch, sh, etc.) and blends (bl, str, etc.) using Alpha to Omega Flashcards available from SENCO (let him/her know your findings).

Is reading a chore or a threat?
- Student may have been forced to read. Encourage student to use books from the library or home that interest them, and at the appropriate reading level. Books to suit a wide range of reading abilities are available for English lessons from English and SEN departments.
- Accessing information may be a hurdle. Make sure the student can use 'contents ' and 'index' pages.

Is there a chance to read with someone?
- Ask student if someone at home can hear/pair or share read with him/her. Fellow tutees, LSAs, or sixth formers can help in college.
- Some texts with accompanying audio-cassettes are available in college or in local libraries.

Is it a question of confidence?
- Make sure the student achieves 90% accuracy.
- Fill in the gaps to encourage fluency when reading one to one. If too many gaps are being filled in, the reading level is inappropriate.
- Check worksheet layouts are clear.

Does the student rely on others to read for him/her?
- If the student always sits next to an able reader, and 'forgets' material, try separating the partnership and observe. If the student then struggles, refer to SENCO for a reading test and advice.

Is the student dyslexic?
- See pages 50, 55.

Figure 9.3 Detailed information and suggestions – basic readers

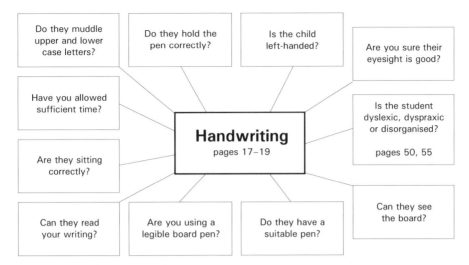

Figure 9.4 Spider diagram – handwriting

Handwriting

The 'nuts and bolts' of handwriting (letter shapes, capitals, keeping on a line, etc.) may need to be re-learnt.

The neatness of handwriting may need to be progressively improved. Neatness usually diminishes when under pressure and with speed. Setting a manageable target of 'x' number of neatly written lines may help. The number of lines can be progressively increased and suitably rewarded.

Do they hold the pen correctly?
- Ideally between thumb and forefinger, resting on the middle finger.
- In a manner in which they have control of the nib.
- Pen grips are available from Special Needs Department if these will help.

Do they have a suitable pen?
- A rollerball is probably the most suitable for writing.
- A pencil should be used for all drawing/diagrams.

Are they sitting correctly?
- Encourage the student to sit upright.
- Students should sit straight onto the board/facing the front where possible.
- All four legs of the chair or stool should be on the floor.

Are you sure their eyesight is good?
- Some students are reluctant to wear glasses if they have been advised to by their Optician. Do they have a pair in the bottom of their bag?
- Perhaps they need a sight test to establish the condition of their eyesight. Suggest to their form tutor/parents and inform SENCO.

Figure 9.5 Detailed information and suggestions – handwriting

Approval or not?

We were anxious that our document should not be seen as threatening but as a useful tool. Having produced a draft copy we distributed it to all interested staff, particularly Heads of Departments, and received very positive responses together with helpful suggestions to take into consideration. We needed to know that it was a workable resource.

What now?

We decided to put a few copies of the document into every department but on reflection this was not ideal. As with every new school initiative (of which we have many!) there are those staff who are more responsive than others. We wanted to know that all interested staff could have access to their own copy and be able to use it readily. Consequently all interested staff were offered a copy and we had a great uptake.

Having taken the initiative we, the Learning Support Department, feel we are 'on board' with literacy initiatives within the college and feel we have played and can continue to play an important part in their development.

Post LITDOC?

Since developing the LITDOC we have been fortunate to have been involved with Maureen Lewis as part of the EXEL project. Maureen has been working with several departments in the College, namely English, Geography, Science, ICT with the Learning Support Department having the overview. Her input has ensured that literacy will continue to be a high priority for us.

Maureen's involvement has provided staff with additional strategies and has given individual departments an opportunity to look more closely at what they are offering and has helped develop more creative ways of presenting materials. All of these ideas we anticipate incorporating into the LITDOC, acknowledging that it is a working document which we hope to extend. Our planned INSET later in October 1999 will enable this. At the time of writing the LITDOC is being updated and we hope that this will be an ongoing process. New ideas from staff are always welcome.

What have we achieved?

- We have produced in-house a document which gives staff security in knowing that they are being supported in exploring different strategies to help overcome student difficulties and also supported in the setting of targets for students across the curriculum.
- We have celebrated success by highlighting good practice across the curriculum.
- We have recognised the professionalism and expertise of our Learning Support team.
- We have created an even stronger Learning Support team by recognising each others' strengths.
- We have made a start in addressing literacy issues within the curriculum in line with the National Literacy Strategy.
- We have been involved with other professionals in developing a way forward.
- We have established a collaborative approach to learning/teaching.
- Literacy is very much on our agenda!

Acknowledgement

The 'LITDOC' was created by all the members of the Learning Support Team: Sarah Kehaya, Linda Hamlin, Jan Houghton, Jo Smith, Barbara Thorp, Wendy Waters, Isobel Western.

Chapter 10

Putting literacy on the secondary agenda

Maggie Croxford and Val McGregor

> The Literacy Project was the single most important initiative in terms of improving the quality of teaching and learning in the school.
>
> (Head of English and Literacy Coordinator)

The Greenwich context

It is important, initially, to put the LEA in context. The London Borough of Greenwich covers an area of less than 20 miles on the outskirts of southeast inner London. In social and economic terms the Borough is one of great contrasts, with pockets of affluence and areas which have high levels of poverty. A high number of children in both primary and secondary schools are eligible for free school meals. The Borough is ranked as the eleventh most deprived LEA out of a total of 366. In some areas due to negative experiences at school themselves, parents do not place a high value on the educational process. The community is culturally diverse. Just over 7,000 pupils (18 per cent) of pupils in our schools speak English as an additional language, with a total of 100 different languages being spoken.

Although results in the Key Stage 2 English tests have been rising in recent years a significant percentage of pupils (about 50 per cent) remain below the national average when they enter Year 7. The 14 secondary schools in the LEA face considerable challenges, therefore, in raising the attainment of these pupils, especially those schools with a high proportion of low attainers. Since 1995 we have attempted to support secondary schools in meeting this challenge. Following a high profile Literacy Conference at one of our secondary schools in July 1995, we set up a Borough Literacy Steering Group and we launched two projects: one focused at primary level and one at secondary level. The initial response from some secondary head teachers was interesting but rather discouraging. They felt that all the available funding should go to their primary colleagues. Whilst welcoming this generosity, we were disappointed that requests for the project came from only three secondary schools in the first year, with one of these schools due to close by the end of the year.

However, these three schools were very eager to be involved and we launched into the project with them enthusiastically. The initial success of the project in these schools glowed like a beacon and thereafter we had no problems with take up.

How the project worked: the structure of the work in schools

We decided to adopt a model of audit and support – aimed at the whole school community. We made a conscious decision to focus on a whole-school approach, rather than a model aimed at providing extra support to a small number of targeted pupils, thereby only involving a minority of staff. We felt it was important to raise awareness at every level and to involve as many staff and students as possible so that literacy became high profile throughout the school.

The audit

The audit was very thorough and looked at the way literacy skills were being addressed across the curriculum. It included: interviews with all heads of departments, the librarian, the SENCO, and, most importantly, students. We also scrutinised a large sample of writing from all subject areas and conducted lesson observation across the curriculum.

We knew how important it was that staff understood the rationale and the scope of the audit so before it took place we explained this at a staff meeting and answered questions. We tried to ensure that the audit was not viewed as an inspection, although this was sometimes how it was perceived. We gave adequate time to the audit and in our largest school this meant both of us being in school for well over a week. We created and used a range of proformas, interview schedules and checklists to support us in the audit. By the end of each audit we had a massive amount of information about the school, with a myriad of perspectives related to language, literacy and learning.

Students' perceptions

Some of the most interesting data came from the students themselves and we always included key quotations from these interviews in the report to each school because they often spoke more powerfully than our findings and evaluations. For example, when asked the amount of reading they did in schools, a Year 8 pupil commented:

'You don't really get to read much at all apart from in English – we never read in other lessons.'

Even more telling was the statement from a Year 10 boy:

'Teachers tell us what to read – but they don't tell us *how* to read it.'

However, many pupils enjoyed and felt supported by group reading activities, well structured research tasks and paired reading. As one Year 8 girl commented, the collaborative nature of reading in a group:

'gives you confidence – we can help each other discover the meaning and learn a lot.'

Students in many schools admitted that they lacked research skills and sometimes tried the tactic of 'turning every other word into your own words', rather than simply copying chunks of text. They admitted freely that they often got print outs from CD-ROMs for homework, 'Because it's easy'; although they were quite aware that they learnt nothing from the process. They expressed frustration when presented with open-ended topics to research:

'Some times teachers say – "Find out about…" And we don't know where to look or how to go about it or what to find out.'

Students were also very forthcoming about the strategies, which did help them in their learning. They knew the value of talk:

'Talking things through helps us to understand. If you only say things in your head it doesn't help – you have to get them out.'

They appreciated the opportunities for pair and group work and felt that 'Discussion always gives you more ideas.' They valued opportunities for talk before tackling writing tasks and in many schools they had perceptive comments to make about the writing process. A great many students of all ages spoke disparagingly about copying: 'It goes from the board onto the page and not through the mind' said one astute girl in Year 9. ' You don't think about what you're writing – you just look at the letters.' They disliked being rushed into copying 'chunks of stuff', which they often admitted they never looked at again. They found planning and drafting helpful approaches but often said these skills were taught only in English.

In all schools there were pockets of excellent practice but it was all too common that practice in one class was not shared sometimes even within the subject – let alone across the school. It was also crystal clear that students themselves did not transfer skills learnt in one lesson to another. So whilst they planned, edited and redrafted pieces of writing with great skill in an English or humanities lesson for example, they did not employ these skills when tackling writing in other subjects. And, of course, they weren't often asked or expected to.

Staff views

The staff interviews were also fascinating to undertake and gave the advisory teacher the opportunity of getting to know many of the staff she was going to work with for the next year. Staff were sometimes extremely reflective and perceptive about the learning environment and we always ensured that their views were incorporated into the report as well. We felt that the main function of the report was to mirror back to the school the views and opinions of its key stakeholders and to indicate where good practice existed and the scope for sharing this.

Staff frequently commented that the school was not conducive to promoting a 'reading culture'. They recognised that good practice in teaching literacy was not shared across the school. They commented on students' reluctance to read, and sometimes admitted to limiting the reading demands: 'We short cut the reading for them', although they were aware that this 'spoon feeding' was not addressing the problem. They felt that students needed a great deal of support in learning how to use language precisely in subjects like Maths, RE and Business Studies. They often commented on students' lack of grammatical knowledge, 'They don't know how to construct sentences.'

Whereas students clearly disliked copying, many staff put forward the opposite view. 'Student love copying – we can't wean them off this.' It was interesting that on many occasions teachers and students held such opposing views. It was clear from an external perspective that had there been better communication between teachers and students, these opposing views could have been resolved.

In all schools it was apparent that many staff, through no fault of their own, did not feel able to teach literacy in their subject especially when students had low reading ages and found writing difficult. But there was an overriding desire to learn and this was one of the key factors in the success of the project. It was our job to exploit this interest and skill up teachers through inset, classroom support, joint planning and co-teaching.

Common themes

There were spectacular examples of literacy teaching in every school. There were classrooms in which language was used so skilfully by teachers that the learning was tangible and dramatic. For example, in geography lessons for Year 8 students, literacy was at the core. Students explored the topic of the Kobe Earthquake through a range of carefully structured literacy activities including: DARTS, managed discussion, structured note-taking, and the use of differentiated writing frames. They were then able to write extended essays on the topic, which were well structured, detailed and in an appropriate style.

However, this teacher's level of awareness of the importance of scaffolds and active approaches to reading and note-taking was rare. Similar themes emerged across all schools and there was a great deal of scope for improvement. Reading activities could be passive rather than active; reading resources sometimes limited and inappropriate, and the teaching of reading was all too frequently seen to be the sole domain of English and SEN departments. Libraries were underused across the curriculum. Note-taking and study skills were constantly required of students but only occasionally modelled or taught.

Copying was too common and dictionaries scarce. Spelling errors were often not corrected and even when they were there was no explicit teaching of spelling. Feedback on students' writing was sometimes inadequate in terms of moving students on as writers. In too many classrooms *at that time* (i.e. before the audit and developmental work) the important link between language and learning was not understood or exploited, and sometimes oracy was undervalued. This picture has, of course, radically changed during the last three years.

The report and advisory teacher support

The detailed report we wrote for each school following the audit included specific curriculum targets for reading, writing, and speaking and listening. In each school we returned with the report and presented this to the staff. Sometimes this was quite difficult and staff resisted the findings. But in each school there was always a core of interested and enthusiastic teachers who responded positively and, provided the senior management team valued and prioritised the project, a good start could be made.

The school was provided with 15 days of advisory teacher time, to work in the school alongside a wide range of groups and individuals within the school community: teachers, classroom assistants, senior managers, heads of department and parents. At the start of the project in each school the advisory teacher provided whole-school INSET on oracy, reading, writing and spelling. This was vitally important. It set the scene, gave the staff a common baseline and ensured a shared agenda and a common language. Equally important was the departmental INSET, which was carried out with all those departments which showed interest and, in most schools, eventually this was every subject department.

Secondary schools are busy and complex organisations and any whole-school initiative risks dilution and burn-out unless there is a constant reminder of its importance. Adopting a 'drip feed' approach has meant that the advisory teacher support often lasted as long as a year so that the profile on literacy has been maintained. Being flexible was also very important. The advisory teacher often visited as many as five schools in a day, in order to fit in with requests to attend particular meetings. More recently this has included lots of evening meetings to launch Family Literacy initiatives.

Teachers are overburdened and sadly rarely receive praise individually on a day to day basis. Therefore the advisory teacher's habit of praising teachers for taking risks in the classroom and undertaking new approaches, has meant that she has been able to win teachers over. Her approach has always been hands on: working alongside them; co-teaching; trialling new approaches to learning; developing language resources with individuals and groups of teachers and, throughout the process, giving teachers the positive feedback they need, if they are to develop new strategies to develop literacy skills and increase learning.

Summer celebratory conferences

The annual summer conferences have been a crucial part of the project. They have provided forums in which we can celebrate school initiatives and share good practice. Senior management groups, individual teachers and departments have been able to tell their stories to a wider audience and this has validated their hard work and inspired those listening. Each year the size of the audience has grown. The advisory teacher now starts working towards the event from the beginning of September, identifying teachers and departments to make presentations and ensuring that all subject areas are represented.

School evaluations

The written evaluations we received during the three years confirmed that the secondary schools liked the approach of audit and advisory teacher support and were particularly appreciative of external advice and guidance. One head teacher reported that:

> Advisory support has been critical for the school. Improvements could not have been made without it. Staff have felt encouraged by the feedback received and she has always acknowledged the successful strategies teachers have used. Staff regarded her as a critical friend. She provided a role model for good practice, inspiring staff and leading them into the belief that involvement in the project would provide them with long-term benefits.

Another commented:

> The project was successful because the advisory teacher was able to translate people's ideas for them. Once they saw that their ideas could work

they were enthusiastic to build on this and to try new strategies . . . people from all curriculum areas felt that improving literacy was a real issue.

The audit too, although sometimes quite hard hitting, was felt to be vital in giving the school a baseline from which to work.

> The report provided us with a great deal of data. It gave us clear targets and a strategy for moving towards a whole-school language policy. We now have such a policy for the first time.

Having been involved in the project from its inception, one head teacher wrote:

> The project has made a significant difference to our school. It brought staff together to work on the issue of learning and to take on a challenge. All staff are now aware of the issues. There is evidence of much more oracy across the curriculum. Children are reading more. Reading ages have improved.

Recent developments

The Skillswork Single Regeneration Budget (SRB) project

The LBG project outlined above came to a close in April 1998, but its success meant that we were in a very favourable position when we became involved in the most recent literacy initiative: a cross-Borough SRB project 'Raising Attainment in Key Stage 3 Literacy', instigated by Skillswork. This focuses on a particular cohort: those pupils entering Year 7 below National Curriculum Level 4. Five LEAs are involved – Bexley, Lewisham, Newham, Tower Hamlets and Greenwich. The project aims to raise the literacy levels of the targeted pupils to average levels by the end of the key stage.

Refocused objectives
The SRB project has given us the opportunity to refocus the literacy work in Greenwich, to concentrate on the under-attainers, especially boys and students with English as an additional language (EAL). Because we have a large percentage of students entering Year 7 below Level 4 this project is crucial to our Borough Literacy Strategy. As Graham Frater says:

> For pupils and schools alike, literacy problems that persist into Key Stage 3 are increasingly hard to deal with. At an age when he (commonly) is becoming clearly aware of falling behind, the Year 7 or Year 8 pupil who has reading difficulties faces a twofold problem: he must catch up and must keep up. And he must do both at exactly the point when, at a faster

rate than he has experienced before, the curriculum makes new demands
on his difficulties . . . Nor is it a matter of working on skills alone; just as
crucially it involves providing for the stock of reading experiences in
which his poor skills have left him deficient.   (Frater 1997)

Although the needs of these students had always been part of our previous project,
we became increasingly aware of the need to home in on this cohort in a more structured way and, because of the whole-school work on literacy within our first project,
we are now able to do this in a very fertile context.

   The project brought with it welcome funding, a large proportion of which we
allocated to schools for resources, salary enhancements, etc., according to the size of
the cohort entering Year 7 below Level 4 in the English Key Stage 2 tests. Whilst the
copious administration of an SRB project is, at times, exceptionally time consuming,
it does create a sense of accountability and responsibility. Expectations of schools
are clearly defined as they are in terms of the LEA support and resource allocation.

   All our 14 secondary schools and four of our special schools with Key Stage 3
pupils are involved in the project. Each secondary school has appointed a literacy
coordinator. These post-holders have been crucial in continuing to keep literacy high
on the schools' agendas. Together they form a formidable and powerful group which
meets on a termly basis to report on progress, decide on future developments and
share ideas. There is a real openness and responsiveness to new ideas and a strong
sense of commitment to a shared agenda. In addition, we have a small steering group
including head teachers, inspectorate and advisory staff and four of the school
coordinators. This group has responsibility for overall management of the project at
LEA level.

Quantitative and curricular targets

In negotiation with the Borough Coordinator (previously the advisory teacher) each
school has now set itself quantitative targets for raising the literacy levels of low
attainers by the end of the key stage for the next three years and curricular targets for
achieving these. The action plans are regularly reviewed and monitored by the
coordinator on school visits.

Tracking targeted students

The SRB cohorts are being tracked in each school. Baseline assessment includes the
use of the NFER Group Reading test for Year 7 and the pupils are re-tested in Year
9. There are formative teacher assessments across the key stage. The assessments are
made initially by teachers in English departments but they are distributed for other
subject teachers to validate. The aim is to ensure that the literacy targets set for these
students become integrated into the teaching in all their classes and to ensure that
staff have some understanding of the English National Curriculum levels, and what
they say about a pupil's reading and writing.

Exciting developments

Several new initiatives have arisen over the last year. These have included the setting up of Family Literacy schemes at secondary level. From a tentative beginning in July 1998, when we were encouraging schools to think about parents evenings focusing on literacy, we have moved to a position where eight of the 14 secondary schools have organised a series of workshop sessions for parents. As yet, the number of parents attending has been small, but all the sessions have been very well received and our intention is to build on these.

We have also provided focused literacy training for classroom assistants – a growing population in Greenwich secondary schools – and these have been exceptionally well received. Head teachers have willingly released staff for this INSET. Another strong theme in the SRB project has been the explicit message to students about the transference of skills across subject boundaries and the need for them to take responsibility for this themselves. The Borough Coordinator has therefore addressed students at assemblies to encourage them to take this on for themselves.

One of our schools was a pilot for the first Summer Literacy Schools in 1997. We were delighted to receive funding in 1998 to run a further four. With some Borough funding, and support from 'Education Extra', we made this stretch to five. We formed a small working group who designed the curriculum for the Summer Schools, which included taking on some of the pedagogy of the literacy hour. This prepared us well for the demands of the 1999 Summer Schools, when we will be organising ten Summer Schools. The Summer School initiative is now seen as an important strand in our overall strategy.

Piloting aspects of the literacy hour

As part of the SRB project we have also run a pilot project in five schools, disseminating the NLS materials, the NLS framework and the structure and pedagogy of the literacy hour. We invited secondary schools to send representatives to the five-day course for intensive schools and then offered them a series of sessions to study the approaches in more depth and think about their application at Key Stage 3.

In one school the SEN department sent representatives to the conference and disseminated the package of materials and ideas, which the department compiled as a result of the INSET. A whole-school INSET day was devoted to literacy and this included discussion of the literacy hour. The SEN staff felt very comfortable with the pedagogy of the literacy hour since they felt it contained many elements they were already using: they are now adopting a modified version of the literacy hour when they withdraw Year 7 and 8 students who have reading ages below 8.3 years. Teachers are successfully using Big Books for the shared reading, a checklist to assess students' phonic knowledge, teaching phonics in a structured, systematic way and using the strategy of guided reading.

In another school, a girls' school with a large number of bilingual pupils, elements of the literacy hour were taken on as a result of working with Maureen Lewis from the Nuffield EXEL Project. Some very interesting work has been achieved. Two English teachers have piloted guided reading in Year 7 and have been very impressed with the way this has accelerated students' progress. (See Chapter 8 for a full account of this work.) Guided reading has replaced silent reading. The teachers feel that they have much more knowledge of the way in which children read. The group tasks introduced have been active and engaging and assisted the teachers in making assessments. 'I now feel I know more about their reading (hearing them talk about reading),' said one of the teachers in a recent interview about the work. The talking about the processes involved in reading has been key to supporting children and to their teachers' assessment of pupils' strengths and weaknesses.

Key factors for success at LEA and school level

We are not claiming that the projects in Greenwich have always been smooth running. There have inevitably been problems, dilemmas, set-backs and frustrations along the way. However, the overall thrust has been positive. We list below what we believe to be key factors for success at LEA level and school level.

LEA level
- Working in partnership with the head teachers of the secondary schools.
- Involving key personnel in schools in management of the project at LEA level.
- Accepting that curriculum changes take a lengthy period of time to embed.
- Anticipating set-backs and not losing sight of the broad picture.
- Celebrating success continuously and formally at the annual summer conferences.
- Embracing a variety of strategies and approaches and 'attacking on all fronts'.
- Attracting external funding.
- Welcoming support from external agencies.

School level
- Commitment of the head teacher and senior management team.
- Whole-school and departmental INSET.
- External support from a flexible coordinator.
- The drip feed nature of the support.
- Recognition of success and positive feedback to departments and individual teachers on a regular basis.
- Making issues explicit to students; encouraging them to transfer their skills.
- Involving the whole school community.

- Accountability for outcomes through the action planning and tracking of students' progress within the SRB project.
- External funding.
- Awareness that school and Borough based concerns are high on the national agenda.

What this means at school level

To demonstrate how the processes outlined above have worked we will conclude by describing the impact of the Borough literacy initiative on individual schools. Each school has adapted the work to meet its particular needs, and although what follows does not provide a *template* for success, it demonstrates how it is essential for the literacy work to be truly embedded into the school's curriculum and policies. Each of the schools has taken a different route in intiating literacy iniatives and we will look at four case studies of individual schools, indicating the variety of approaches and methodology they successfully used.

School 1 Commitment and creativity

As has already been suggested, the early days of the project were not overwhelmingly positive: the secondary schools did not believe that teaching literacy was their responsibility. Fortunately, the head teacher of a mixed Catholic school did not agree, and this school was the first to participate. The school has had exciting and lasting results, both in terms of continuous raised achievement and increased awareness of staff.

The particular factors that contributed to the success of this school, were the extraordinary commitment of the senior management team, in particular the head teacher, the willingness to work with other outside agencies focusing on literacy, and lastly, the interest and creativity of individual staff. From the outset, the head teacher decided that literacy would be the focus of the school's work, believing, and regularly restating his view, that it was the key to achievement. To this end, he welcomed the rigorous literacy audit of the school, and once this was completed, embarked upon a detailed plan for tackling the issues raised. As in many cases, the audit highlighted reading as a key issue. This was particularly pertinent as a significant number of boys were apparently not reading at all. It was decided to introduce a paired reading/ mentor scheme, pairing Year 10 and 11 pupils with Year 7 and 8. Initially, the block-timetabled pastoral period was used for this. However, some staff felt uneasy about aspects of PSHE not being covered, and so it was decided that 'a reading period' should be instituted for Year 7. Added to this, a PACT scheme was initiated, called 'Reading Together', which allowed the reading mentors in school, family members at home and younger pupils to read together and conduct a dialogue about the process.

Each year, at the 'transition meeting' for parents, before the new Year 7 join the school, the senior teacher in charge of literacy launches this scheme, with the help of local libraries, a local bookseller and the advisory teacher. Parental support has been excellent, and the students have seen this as an opportunity to get involved with their secondary school before transfer. The head teacher reported enthusiastically to the advisory teacher

> 'There's definitely a real reading culture in the school now . . . when I walk along the corridors during the day, students are hunched over books and talking about books . . . even the boys!'

This focus on reading, coupled with a complete overhaul of the library and its entire stock, resulted in a significant increase in the amount, quality and frequency of the reading done throughout the school. Currently, the whole school is involved in the reading mentor scheme: Years 7 and 8 being supported by Years 9, 10 and 11.

In addition, many key staff in a range of departments have trialled a variety of literacy strategies in their subject areas. For example, the Humanities department, having attended an INSET delivered by Maureen Lewis on writing frames and the EXIT model, decided to use these strategies in History and Geography. The Religious Education teacher also attended an eight-week course on literacy and learning, which enhanced her planning and curriculum development. The Art department began to look at ways of formalising pupils evaluating their art work with another student, or capturing these discussions on tape. The Science and Maths departments also decided to focus upon oracy, and began work at Key Stage 3, and in particular Year 9. The Science department focused upon the role of teacher prompting in group discussions, and Maths looked at the role of talk in enhancing investigations. Students began to notice distinct differences in approaches in classrooms.

The interest in oracy led the school to be involved with a project, organised between Cambridge University and Greenwich, called 'Taste'; a cross-phase initiative designed to develop storytelling as a tool for learning across the curriculum. This, in turn, has led to other departments, most notably Technology, also developing interesting oral strategies to enhance learning. For example, they have been exploring ways in which the use of narrative and storytelling can enhance understanding and memorising.

All these initiatives and developments have resulted in a wider range of teaching strategies being used, more coherence across the school, and, most importantly, raised achievement. The school revisited and redrafted its whole-school literacy policy, and each year they invite the inspector or the advisory teacher to re-audit the school in order to monitor progress in literacy: they aim to continue this process.

School 2 Powerful beginnings – rapid outcomes

The second school, a mixed secondary school, had a difficult start with their literacy work as the staff reacted very negatively to the literacy audit, which contained some serious criticisms of the teaching and learning strategies used within the school. This school has now made a significant contribution to the literacy work in the Borough. This school adopted a very different, but equally successful approach to the first implementation. Once again, the senior management, and in particular the head teacher, were instrumental in the school's success. The school appointed an additional member to the senior management team, whose responsibility was 'teaching and learning'. Within this brief, the senior teacher arranged a two-day whole-school INSET focusing on all aspects of literacy: oracy, reading and writing. Workshop sessions were run for all faculties on writing frames and reading within their subjects. The Borough Reading Recovery tutor led a session on intervention strategies, and the advisory teacher led whole-school sessions on oracy and learning and issues surrounding reading in the secondary curriculum. The impact of these INSET days was tremendous: the staff embraced the strategies across the curriculum instantly. Those most in evidence are: spelling strategies and the teaching of key words; using word-boxes and writing frames to enhance writing; and, lastly, but perhaps most significantly, oral strategies and the management of pupil groupings.

The school has quickly developed an in-depth language and learning policy arising from these developments. The Literacy Steering Group continues to meet regularly, at least twice per half term, to monitor the progress of work in classrooms. These meetings are a major factor in the success of the school: they are very short (lasting about 30 minutes during a lunch-break, with refreshments provided), focused and positive. They provide a regular forum for cross-curricular discussions and, most importantly, ensure that literacy issues are constantly on the school's agenda.

Most recently, this steering group has identified and organised a team of Year 12 reading tutors, who have been trained by the advisory teacher. This group now has reading tutees, with which they meet at mutually convenient times. They keep records on the younger pupils, identify their needs and develop reading programmes. This has been very successful, both in developing and promoting reading within the school, but also in establishing positive links between the lower school and the sixth form.

School 3 Refocusing and developing autonomy

The third school that we wish to highlight is also a mixed secondary school, but at the south end of the Borough. Their initial approach was not dissimilar to that followed by the previous two schools, however the initial impact was far less sustained. Unfortunately, the momentum of the work within the school was interrupted by an

OFSTED inspection. However, the school had been invited to provide the main display for the annual literacy celebratory conference, and the creation of this and sharing of the good practice that emerged, gave the staff a renewed positive stance towards their work on literacy. The display also provided a public forum for the school's beliefs about, and strategies for, literacy. Nevertheless, the school still felt the need to revisit classroom practice, in order to get a clearer picture of the teaching and learning strategies being employed. It was decided that to facilitate this, the school would use the funding from the SRB budget to pay for three key staff, the Head of English, the Literacy Coordinator and the SENCO, to meet for two periods (one hour and a half hour) each week. This has proved to be extremely successful. The key staff have the opportunity to discuss future plans, monitor the progress of the literacy action plan and to share materials and resources. This signals to staff the value of literacy within the school's agenda.

One of the most significant decisions to emerge from this management group, was the re-audit of the school. It was clear that good literacy practices were less evident than previously, and it was felt that an internal audit, conducted by the three senior managers of the project, would be a focused but relatively non-threatening way of ascertaining classroom practice and a useful second stage, following the previous external audit. In fact, the audit had three phases: a detailed audit of pupils' writing, classroom observations and a brief update on departmental statements on literacy. This strategy was effective for the following reasons: the school conducted the audit themselves and were, therefore, able to view real day to day classroom practice; the management team was able to gain an updated view of the state of practice; and, lastly, the ensuing recommendations were monitored by the team, on a day to day basis. It was clear that, without the time for the managers to meet, this audit would not have occurred, and certainly would not have been followed up so thoroughly.

Indeed, in view of this success, despite the cost of the timetabled meetings, the school has decided to continue the practice for, at least, the next academic year.

School 4 The English department take the lead

The fourth school, that offers a further alternative model of literacy development, was a single-sex girls' school, with a significant number of pupils with EAL. The initial audit process and early development work was similar to the other schools in the initial stages. However, the distinguishing feature of this school was that, contrary to our belief, starting with the English department, provided that there is sufficient senior management support and respect for the English staff, can, in particular circumstances, be a very effective strategy.

With the support of the advisory teacher, the English department began developing writing frames and formulating a spelling policy. The English department then disseminated its work. It did this in two ways: firstly, they installed a range of generic writing frames on the school network; secondly, after developing a structured approach to spelling which they had used with a range of pupils, they led whole-school INSET on spelling strategies.

The EAL department was also keen to participate with the literacy developments. Obviously, they saw that the issues were similar but they were anxious to focus on the particular needs of bilingual pupils. In order to do this, one EAL teacher, with the help of the advisory teacher, developed an excellent booklet designed to support EAL pupils when doing research. This has proved to be an invaluable resource for the school, equally supportive of pupils and to staff in other curriculum areas. Moreover, this resource was then made available to other schools, both within and outside the Borough. This was the first publication to be completed by a school, and disseminated in this way. Needless to say, many other schools in the Borough, have designed and compiled texts and resources, supporting literacy; all of which have now been shared and developed borough-wide.

In conclusion, although the issue of individuality and variety of approaches to meet schools' specific needs and interests is key; it is quite clear that over a period of time the same issues are covered in every school. We are continuing our work on raising literacy standards within the Borough but we are encouraged by the progress that has already been made and the commitment that has been shown by Greenwich teachers.

Chapter 11

A whole-school literacy policy – making it work

Maureen Lewis and David Wray

All secondary schools in England have been made aware of the priority the current government is giving to the issue of supporting literacy within Key Stage 3 and as the preceding chapters have shown these issues are being addressed at LEA, school and departmental level. Some schools will already have well developed action plans and policy statements but the current expectations are that all schools should be involved. The final overhead transparency of the two-day literacy conferences in the Summer term of 1999 listed the following post conference expectations for all schools:

- Delegates should report back to staff and governors at the earliest opportunity on issues arising from the conferences and their implications for the school.
- A properly representative literacy management group should review the school's position regarding literacy and formulate proposals for action where this is needed.
- The school should aim to set aside at least one closure day in 1999/2000 for staff training to support the school's literacy initiative.
- The school should be in a position to explain its policy regarding literacy provision in the event of a LEA review or OFSTED inspection.
- LEA staff will discuss with schools how it intends to support literacy development at Key Stage 3, within the terms of its educational development plan.

(OHT 12, LEA conference file, DfEE 1999b)

Delegates returning to school, to report back on their conference experiences and to begin to consider the next steps, returned to institutions with very different starting points. Each secondary school represents a unique context. Context-specific factors might include the socio-economic status of the pupils, the type of school, the location of the school, the school's view of itself as failing or succeeding and the history and culture of the school (Reynolds 1998, p. 157). These factors will influence the actions the school takes and may have some influence upon the success or otherwise of initiatives. In formulating its 'proposals for action', however, there is a wealth of research evidence and examples of good practice that schools can draw upon. In this final chapter we will consider the elements that should be included within a school's literacy action plan; look at the implementation cycle; consider the factors identified by school effectiveness research that can influence the successful implementation of a literacy policy and finally look at the problems involved in implementing *lasting* change in schools.

A multi-stranded approach

There appear to be four main areas of potential development in literacy work for schools to consider:

1. The specific teaching of literacy within English and related departments such as special needs and language support departments (e.g. the teaching of reading, the possible use of the Year 7 framework and a literacy hour, the role of the SEN department, the value of individualised integrated learning systems).
2. The subject-specific literacy demands within individual departments (e.g. the teaching of subject-specific vocabulary, the reading demands of different subject texts, how writing demands might vary in different subjects).
3. Cross-curricular issues of literacy which can be supported by all departments (e.g. whole-school spelling and marking policies, widening the range of text on offer, the use of shared and modelled reading and writing opportunities; the use of individualised literacy targets/diaries for pupils which are used across departments).
4. A whole-school literacy awareness strand that concentrates on creating and maintaining a positive ethos towards literacy and a high public profile for literacy within the institution (e.g. whole-school literacy events such as book days, a 'literacy rich environment' school display policy, literacy reward schemes, 'buddy' reading schemes).

Each of these four elements can be regarded as both a separate and/or an inter-woven strand but a multi-strategy approach has been promoted and has been judged to be a factor in those schools with successful literacy initiatives (DfEE 1999b).

Curriculum development cycles

There are no shortage of detailed and persuasive models for the necessary steps needed to implement a whole-school literacy curriculum development cycle (see for example Webster *et al.* 1996, Catron 1997, Bearne 1999). Most of these models share several common features and move through a process characterised by the following, often recurrent, stages:

(a) Identify members for a school 'literacy group' to manage the initiative.
(b) Establish a database of current practice via audit and pupil tracking.
(c) Analyse strengths and needs based on audit evidence.
(d) Decide on priorities, set first targets.
(e) Develop specific, public action plan with clear areas of responsibility, budgets, targets, dates and success criteria.
(f) Initiate action/begin to prepare brief policy documents.
(g) Monitor and evaluate, report back to whole school.
(h) Refine action plans and policy documents as result of monitoring/evaluation.
(i) Consolidate current phase and initiate next phase.

These, or similar cycles of activity, have begun in many schools and a typical proforma for an initial action plan is shown in Figure 11.1. The items in this plan were chosen as being relatively easy for all staff to initiate and likely to offer some early success. Starting in this way is important for several reasons which are outlined below in the sections on 'Key success factors' and 'Implementing change' but early, inclusive action rather than a lengthy, document-producing phase can have a strong impact on staff and student motivation.

However, even if schools have undertaken an audit and have drawn up an action plan and monitored its progress, these are not in themselves sufficient to ensure that an initiative is successful or becomes a truly integrated feature of school life. In order for this to happen there is a complex range of factors which need to be considered. Fortunately there is growing evidence and consistent advice for schools from a variety of sources (DfEE, school effectiveness and literacy researchers, HMI reports) concerning the factors which may influence the success and long-term impact of a literacy initiative. These factors include management issues, teaching and learning issues, ethos and attitude issues and an informed understanding of current practice within the school linked to a planned programme for improvement and change. We will now look in more detail at some of these key 'success' factors.

Key success factors

There is a broad consistency on universal factors that can make a difference to teaching and learning. Sammons *et al.* (1995) identified 11 key features of effective schools drawn from an examination of over 150 studies and Reynolds (1998) draws up a similar list based on an extensive literature review. 'Effectiveness' factors are also identified in the most recent studies on effective literacy teaching (Wragg *et al.* 1998, Medwell *et al.* 1998). Whilst any such list cannot provide a recipe to be applied

Figure 11.1 Literacy plan: Stage 1 – immediate actions

What	Target group	When	How	Person responsible	Training	Budget – what for?	Outcome to be monitored
Buddy reading Intervention strategy	Year 8 Initially Level 3 and below. Possibility of extending to other years	From Sept. 1999 Volunteer mentors (older pupils and adults)	Lunch hours, Monday to Thursday Half an hour	D Shenton D Cushing N Piper R Boarder	Initially M Lewis	Suitable readers Log books Incentive letters	Re-testing 6 months on. Feedback from all parties
Creating a literacy rich environment (display)	All departments	Autumn Term 1999 – subject displays New intake Welcome Sept. 2000 – all entrances	Subject teams half a day INSET Collapsed timetable Year groups during July 2000	C Davies C Aitken N Williams F Stevenson N Rodgers	Visit Middle Schools	Materials INSET Cover costs	Staff and student feedback
Literacy event	Whole school	Spring Term 2000	Collapse timetable for X day(s) Range of events	C Ehrenberg LMG	Unknown	Unknown	Staff student feedback
Extended reading homework	All departments	Autumn Term 1999 onwards	Weekly dedicated reading homework set by each department in turn plus response task. Possibly leading to a cross-curricular reading display for Library and entrance foyer.	V Carah C Ehrenberg		Purchase of extra books Photocopying	Reading gaining higher profile
Parental involvement	All parents but particularly Year 8	Autumn Term onwards	Website, email, billboard Contact Book Involve literacy event Log books Parent buddies?	IT team LMG as relevant		Modification of Contact Books	Parental interest and support
Involve departments in building literacy strategies into their teaching. Start with key words and note-taking leading to other strategies as identified by the audit and departments	All departments	Autumn Term onwards	INSET 6 September then department planning meetings.	C Ehrenberg + subject coordinators. Eventually all staff	INSET 6 Sept M Lewis Ongoing INSET Section meetings led by coordinators initially using NLS video and proforma	INSET	Increased student access to curriculum. Behaviour improvement. Student engagement in learning. Eventually exam results

wholesale, the major factors apparent in effective schools and effective teaching of literacy research include:

- effective and purposeful leadership;
- shared goals within the school/classroom community;
- the creation of a learning environment;
- a concentration on teaching and learning;
- purposeful teaching with clear learning objectives;
- high expectations;
- giving positive reinforcement;
- ensuring progress is monitored;
- recognising pupils' rights and responsibilities;
- developing home, school and community partnerships;
- supporting the professional and pedagogical needs of staff.

(based on Sammons *et al.* 1995, p. 8)

We will discuss each of these factors but in doing so we must also bear in mind, as mentioned previously, that schools are unique, individual organisations as well as organisations that share certain common characteristics with other schools. In introducing a literacy strategy schools must be sensitive to their local situations.

Shared vision and goals

(a) Audits

Defining the problem is an essential first step in implementing a successful literacy policy. An understanding of the school's starting point can be obtained by under-taking the kind of whole-school, departmental and individual audits already mentioned and by making use of the evidence to define target groups for any initiative. Audits have both an information gathering and a consciousness raising impact, both of which can have an important role in developing a shared vision and goals within the school community.

A detailed proforma for a literacy audit, created by Sheffield City Council, was given as a model in the conference materials at the Summer KS3 Literacy Conferences (DfEE 1999b, p. 76–90). It begins by comparing a school's literacy results to the national picture and by examining the general attitude of pupils towards reading and writing. This audit then focuses in upon specific aspects of literacy, the attainment of specific groups of pupils, the management of literacy including staffing and resources, monitoring and assessment and the involvement of parents and governors. Its thoroughness gives a useful model to schools but many schools have found it valuable to draw up their own audits that can be seen to include elements of particular relevance to their context. Figure 11.2 shows an extract from the audit completed by all members of staff in a Devon school, and then collated at both departmental and school level.

Section 6: Teaching strategies

Thinking of the youngest year group you teach, do you use any of the following strategies? If a strategy is unknown to you please indicate.

	rarely	sometimes	often	unknown
Get pupils to copy your notes into their books				
You read aloud to pupils from their text book				
You read aloud to pupils from non text books about your subject				
You provide graphic clues as prompts for specific vocabulary				
Introduce key vocabulary to pupils				
Model, yourself, how to write a particular piece of work				
Encourage rough drafting of a piece of writing				
Check the readability level of texts you give to pupils				
Give differentiated tasks according to pupils' *literacy* skills				
Explicitly teach reading techniques such as skimming and scanning				
Use brainstorming or concept mapping				
Comment positively on literacy when marking students work (e.g. spelling, handwriting)				
Teach spelling strategies				
Have 'library' books as well as text books in teaching rooms				
Use CD-ROMs or other IT based resources				
Set reading as a dedicated homework task				
Use writing frames to prompt writing				
Have specific tasks to encourage speaking and listening				
Model study skills such as note-taking				
Have dictionaries and/or spellcheckers in class				
Have subject-specific dictionaries available in class				
Students undertake cloze procedure (filling in missing words)				
Students undertake text restructuring (showing the information in some other way, e.g. grid)				
Students undertake text sequencing (re-ordering jumbled text)				
Students undertake text prediction (read part then predict before reading on, to check)				

NB The terms 'rarely', 'sometimes', 'often' and 'unknown' were defined at the start of the questionnaire and used consistently throughout.

Figure 11.2 Teaching strategies audit

Like the Sheffield proforma, this audit was inevitably a lengthy and detailed document which demanded some commitment from staff in filling it in. However in completing it, individual staff began to reflect on their own existing practice, departments could get an overview of their strengths and weaknesses and areas of staff development were identified. After committing time to the survey staff were keen to receive the results (which were given and debated at a whole-school meeting) and consider ways forward. The beginnings of a 'shared understanding and goals' culture was started. The opportunity to express anonymously any negative comments, doubts and concerns in the survey also gave the literacy steering group who had drawn up the survey some indications of potential problem areas and resistance to change that they would encounter.

(b) Literacy steering groups

The creation of a shared vision and goal can be developed via the setting up of a school literacy committee with representatives from every department. Such committees have two key roles: to initiate and lead literacy development and to work towards the creation of a written whole-school policy. HMI have identified the importance of formalising literacy initiatives into a public 'institutionalised' policy document as an element apparent in those secondary schools they deemed to be effective in supporting literacy (Robinson and Hertrich 1998). The key here may not be the document itself, but rather the process involved in creating such a document, which demands collaboration across departments. Shared goals are thereby made explicit and it is more likely that departments and teachers will have more than a token allegiance to them if they have had a hand in drawing them up.

From our own observations in schools we would add a further dimension to the work of more successful literacy committees. They have a role in keeping literacy at the forefront of colleagues' minds. Secondary schools are busy institutions and it is usual to have several initiatives running simultaneously. The literacy committee can constantly refocus colleagues' minds upon their shared literacy vision and literacy aims. This might be via a monthly literacy newsletter to all staff, via a regular slot at whole-school staff meetings, through organising literacy events such as author visits and book fairs or by planning a programme of INSET sessions.

The monthly literacy newsletter, circulated to all staff, is a simple but effective method of keeping in touch (See Figure 11.3). Good practice can be shared by asking staff to write up their successful ideas, and encouraging evidence such as improved test scores, positive comments from pupils and so on can be shared. In one school the head teacher added excitement to the newsletter by awarding a prize (a bottle of wine) to the department or individual who came up with the best literacy idea/news item each month. Such tangible (if light-hearted) evidence of the head teacher's involvement leads us to the next key factor – leadership.

Literacy latest

Following my last flier I had lots of very irate Mathematicians beating a path to my door. Very interesting things are going on in Maths, but they are SHY and don't like to be talked about in public! So someone in the Maths department had a prize in their pigeon hole! There were some stunning ideas too. What about shape poems (triangular, circular, etc.)? We could *all* have a go at *subject poems*. How about giving it as a homework task? I'll put up a display of the best. Prizes to the best (teacher or pupil?). Also shape words, verbs and nouns. I hear a certain Mr AR has also tried this idea in Graphics. Well done.

e.g. **TEAR TRIANGLE**

I hear that some videoing went on of some talking in Science. Can we see it, please?

Figure 11.3 Literacy newsletter

Leadership

Involvement of the senior management team is another vital factor in determining the likely success or failure of any initiative (Gray 1990, Caul 1994, Fullan 1991). Professional leadership has been characterised by:

- a participative approach;
- being firm and purposeful;
- providing a model of a leading professional rather than just an administrator.

(Sammons *et al.* 1995, p. 9)

This does not necessarily mean that a head teacher must personally lead a literacy initiative. Most effective heads are able to delegate responsibility (Caul 1994) but they must be seen to give status and support to initiatives. Without this status it is less likely any initiative will be long-lasting. The enthusiasm of a lone individual or small group without high status within the school is usually not enough to sustain an initiative over time. There are a number of ways in which status can be signalled, such as by the designation of the literacy coordinator as a member of the senior management team, the allocation of a specific budget to support the initiative, public support by the head for the work of the literacy coordinator and/or committee, and a lead from the head in encouraging liaison when appropriate with outside agencies that may offer support such as LEAs, universities and consultants (Weindling 1989).

The learning environment

The impact of the learning environment upon the successful implementation of a literacy policy cannot be separated from the impact of the learning environment upon the ethos of the school generally. Factors which enhance learning will enhance literacy learning. However, we can identify a particular literacy dimension within the school environment. Both the creation of an orderly atmosphere and the physical environment of the school help create an effective learning environment (Sammons *et al.* 1995). The Effective Teachers of Literacy project (Medwell *et al.* 1998) also identified the importance of creating 'literate environments' in classrooms. In secondary schools, creating an attractive, literate, working environment might include ensuring that all classrooms (not just English classrooms) are seen as places where literacy is supported. This might include the provision of literacy materials such as word banks and dictionaries, the range of books on offer, the types of displays created, the layout of the room to ensure pupils can see the board/OHP, and so on. Other practical measures include the creation of a print rich environment via displays in the public areas and corridors; the provision of attractive reading materials in public waiting areas: the celebration of literacy via book choice boards, and literacy promotion and book posters around the whole school. The Basic Skills Agency, for example, has a series of posters showing positive images of literacy which feature people of all ages from a range of social and ethnic backgrounds involved in reading and writing activities. The environment of the library (and the range and physical state of its materials) should be considered, as should the use made by pupils of the library. Valuing the literacy environment gives many subtle messages about the importance of literacy and its status within the school community and the wider world and so the inclusion of a section on literacy display policy should be included in a whole-school literacy policy. Some schools have made the creation of literacy rich displays one of the termly targets for every department.

Concentration on teaching and learning

The importance of looking at teaching and learning within a literacy strategy is obvious. Many studies have shown a correlation between such a concentration and school and teacher effectiveness (Mortimore 1993, Creemers 1994). In literacy, approaches to teaching such as teacher modelling and teacher guided reading and writing (as used in the primary National Literacy Strategy) are still new to many secondary teachers. The active literacy teaching strategies exemplified in DARTs activities and the work of the EXEL project (Wray and Lewis 1997) are still only used by a minority of secondary teachers (Lewis and Wray 1999). Attempts to establish a literacy initiative must therefore address directly issues of teaching and learning. These issues have been discussed throughout the book and in particular in Chapter 2.

Visits to local primary schools to see at first hand teaching strategies such as modelled and shared reading and writing have already been suggested as useful in helping subject specialists to see how literacy links with teaching and learning. Within secondary schools, observations by less experienced or confident teachers of the lessons of colleagues who already demonstrate good practice can be powerful. Video materials showing the literacy dimensions of subject teaching can also be used, for example the video provided with the KS3 conference materials and materials produced locally by LEAs. Some schools have also appointed staff literacy mentors – experienced colleagues who are happy to offer advice and support to colleagues.

Purposeful teaching

Quality teaching is clearly at 'the heart of effective schooling' (Sammons *et al.* 1995, p. 15). High quality teaching can be characterised by several factors, one of which is clarity of purpose (NREL 1990). Making the literacy objective of a lesson explicit helps do this. Schools that have embarked upon a literacy development strategy almost inevitably find that eventually departments are involved in revisiting schemes of work and identifying specific literacy and learning objectives within their planning. Figure 7.2 in Chapter 7 shows an example of a Science department planning document which includes stated literacy objectives.

High expectations

While positive expectations of pupil achievement have been identified as one of the most important characteristics of effective schools (United States Department of Education 1987) the link between teacher expectations and pupil achievement is not simple. Expectations do not directly impact upon pupil achievement. Rather, the attitude of teachers may impact upon pupil self-esteem (Bandura 1992), influence the content of lessons (Tizard *et al.* 1988) and act upon teachers themselves by enabling them to feel that they can exercise some control over pupils' difficulties through an active teaching role (Mortimore 1994).

Within the context of a literacy strategy these insights from research highlight the importance of secondary teachers having a clear understanding of the literacy achievements of individual pupils and an understanding of what standards a literate 12-year-old should be achieving. This has several practical consequences. One is that literacy information on individual pupils must be made available to all teachers. A second is that secondary staff should know what a Level 4 in English (the average for an 11-year-old) represents in practical terms. In one of the DfEE 'Standards' funded KS3 pilot literacy projects, this knowledge is introduced to staff by getting teachers from all departments to undertake a Year 6 SAT test and to compare their own results with those of pupils assessed at different levels. Many secondary teachers are surprised at what is demanded and recognise that their own expectations of their pupils may have been too low.

The QCA annual reports on 'Standards in English' at Key Stages 2 and 3 (QCA 1998) differentiates between pupils achieving Levels 3, 4 and 5 using the following criteria.

Children achieving Level 3:
- can retrieve direct information and evidence from a text but not explain its relevance;
- can use commas in lists but not to mark sentence structure;
- need systematic teaching of spelling rules and conventions so that they that they use more than simple sound-letter correspondences and knowledge of familiar words when writing;
- do not use speech marks confidently;
- do not use paragraphs; their sequencing of narrative is not secure, as they have moved beyond simple plots, but they do not have a clear grasp of what the overall structure of their narrative or non-narrative piece might be.

Children achieving Level 4:
- do not use spelling patterns consistently, and have particular problems with vowel phonemes: e.g. special, *carriages*, journey;
- generally use speech marks but punctuation and layout of dialogue is under-developed;
- do not use commas consistently for marking clauses and parentheses, and are insecure in using the possessive apostrophe;
- should structure their writing to make it coherent for the reader, using connectives and subordination; and use structure and distinctive features of different types of non-narrative writing more easily;
- explain inferences and the importance or relevance of textual reference, but do not expand their explanations or identify effects of language use;
- can relate an image to an idea but not evaluate its effect;
- begin to extend their responses but lack specific vocabulary for expressing their ideas.

Children achieving Level 5:
- need to be encouraged to use more sophisticated vocabulary in writing about their reading, particularly to give a personal response to the text as a whole;
- need to extend their understanding of how layout and presentation relate to the purpose and function of texts.

Subject departments could profitably analyse a sample of pupils' written scripts to identify examples of these specific features and consider how they might work on improving them within their lessons.

One outcome of the explicit nature of the teaching objectives in the National Literacy Strategy Framework (DfEE 1998c) has been that what should be expected of a Year 6 pupil is now available for all to see. For some primary teachers this has caused a reassessment of their expectations of pupils. This may be one reason why some secondary schools are now beginning to look at the Framework of Teaching Objectives suggested for Year 7 (see Appendix 2).

Positive reinforcement

Strategies to increase pupils' motivation and self-esteem are a major factor in influencing achievement (Bandura 1992). Low levels of literacy are often associated with low self-esteem, with such pupils tending to consider themselves stupid and unable to progress with literacy. Many secondary schools have introduced literacy award schemes (for example, being offered privileges in return for reading a certain number of books). The impact of such schemes appears to lie in the positive reinforcement they can offer pupils. Other schools have introduced literacy mentors who spend time talking to individual pupils about their literacy, hearing them read, helping them to set individual targets and monitor their own progress. This is helpful not only in providing opportunities for positive feedback but also in making the pupils active participants in the process. Giving pupils some responsibility for (Rutter *et al.* 1979) and some control over their work (Brookover 1979) appear to be significant in motivating pupils. Literacy mentors are drawn from staff or older pupil volunteers and this scheme has the dual advantage of not only raising the self-esteem of the pupil being mentored but it can also positively impact upon the mentor.

Positive, rather than negative, feedback also needs to be addressed when looking at school assessment, marking and spelling policies. One of the DfEE 'Standards' funded KS3 pilot projects has been exploring the use of an assessment instrument for plotting literacy development across the curriculum based on the idea of the 'positive statement banks' first suggested by Birmingham LEA Assessment Unit (Winchester 1995). This is discussed in Chapter 4. Similarly, marking of spelling and punctuation could start from looking at what pupils can do and then building on that.

School-wide prompt charts (see Figure 11.4) can remind pupils of what they can do to help themselves first. In making possible processes explicit to pupils, such charts offer opportunities to support independent learning and to heighten pupils' level of metacognitive awareness.

Not sure how to spell a word?
Have you tried these ways to help yourself?

- Sound out the word
- Think about how it looks
- Think about a similar word
- Is there a memory sentence for this word? (e.g. **b**ig **e**lephants **c**annot **a**lways **u**se **s**mall **e**xits)
- Find the word in a list –
      key words list
      frequently used words list
      your own word bank
- Look it up in a dictionary/spellchecker
- Ask a friend or teacher

Once you've solved it, don't forget to add the correct spelling to your own word bank if it's a word you think will be useful at other times.

Figure 11.4   School-wide prompt chart

Monitoring and evaluating

If a school has a shared set of goals and expectations concerning literacy, it becomes possible to set targets and monitor how both the school as a whole, departments and individual pupils have moved towards such targets. Such monitoring appears to be important in that it focuses the attention of staff, pupils and parents upon the goals. It can also inform, and make more effective, future planning and can help create an ethos that regards these goals as important and worthwhile (Scheerens 1992, Lezotte 1989). At a school level this entails a clear literacy development plan, with identifiable targets, a success indicator, a time scale for action and a key person or department identified as being responsible for initiating action. At an individual pupil level it may involve literacy logbooks for targeted pupils in which their individual or group targets are recorded, positive feedback given by teachers and mentors and progress reviewed. Teachers, mentors, pupils and parents can play their role in this monitoring and evaluating by adding their comments of how far goals have been achieved.

Home–school partnership

The positive effects of supportive relationships and cooperation between schools and parents have been demonstrated in much school effectiveness research. Experience and research based in primary schools has strongly suggested that parental involvement, particularly in reading work, can have a significant impact upon pupils' literacy development (Tizard *et al.* 1982, Topping and Wolfendale 1985). There is growing evidence that the extension of this kind of work to secondary schools can pay dividends (Higgins 1995, Wray and Rogers 1997).

Secondary schools can enlist parents' help in setting targets for their children, can offer parent evenings devoted to literacy and can keep parents informed of their child's literacy progress at frequent, rather than yearly, intervals. Regular meetings with a literacy focus can signal to parents the importance the school is placing upon literacy and offer practical ideas and support for positive parental involvement. In Chapter 10 the introduction of such literacy meetings for parents is described. A measure of the impact of such meetings can be found in Newham's Key Stage 3 pilot project. One school in the Borough implemented a series of literacy meetings for parents. At the first meeting few books were bought from the on site bookshop provided for the evening. By the third meeting over 150 books were bought by parents for their offspring. Other schools have produced leaflets and booklets for parents explaining how they can help at home.

Some schools have widened the involvement of others to include the local business and sporting communities. Industry mentors can help pupils see the importance of literacy in the world of work and the involvement of local sporting heroes can give status to a literacy initiative. In many cities and towns throughout the country, for example in Bristol, the local football club has been involved in schemes to promote literacy within schools. Such projects take literacy beyond the confines of the school and offer powerful models for the importance of literacy in everyday life.

Learning environment/staff development

It seems obvious that effective teachers need to be learners as well as teachers – keeping up to date both in their subject and with new understandings about how pupils learn. On several occasions throughout this book we have raised the issue of training needs and we have already indicated that three quarters of the secondary teachers questioned in our survey (Lewis and Wray 1999) said they had received little (31.7 per cent had had one lecture) or no (44.3 per cent) mention of literacy teaching during their initial teacher training courses. The need for focused in-service courses on literacy is apparent from such findings.

However, research studies that have examined staff development have generally concluded that in-service training 'needs to be school based if it is to have a lasting impact' (Sammons *et al.* 1995, p. 23). The most effective INSET would appear to be ongoing and focused upon improving classroom practice; that is, theory is embedded in or clearly linked to classroom practice.

In the schools in which we have been working the in-service model has been that of school-based, whole staff sessions followed by departmental development sessions over several weeks which have looked at the literacy demands of a specific unit of work. This culminates in a revised unit of work being taught and evaluated for its impact upon student learning and literacy. The members of staff involved then report back to the rest of the staff on what they have done. In this way, new ideas are shared; literacy as a 'theme' is constantly revised within the school and the existing expertise of staff is acknowledged and built upon. Such a model of INSET and development is expensive and time consuming. However, there are many studies that show that one-off presentations by outside experts, although well received on the day, can have a limited long-term impact (Fullan 1991). Improving schools, including improving literacy within schools, is a long-term rather than a short-term project and needs to be properly funded if the most effective forms of INSET are to be encouraged.

Implementing change

In the sections above we have outlined the factors that might make the difference between a literacy initiative being successful or rapidly running out of steam. As we pointed out in Chapter 1, the 'Language Across the Curriculum' initiatives springing from the Bullock Report had only a limited impact in changing the perceptions and practices of secondary school teachers. Consideration of institutional factors which influence lasting change as opposed to short-term change need to be built into any new language across the curriculum initiatives. Fullan (1988, p. 17) has suggested that for successful change to take place there are three essential phases and within each phase he identifies several key requirements (see Figure 11.5).

Stage	Factors
Initiation	• educational needs linked to an agenda of political (high status) need • a clear model for the proposed change • a strong advocate for change • an early active initiation establishing initial commitment (*an elaborate planning stage is wasteful of energy*)
Implementation	• careful orchestration; a group with a clear direction is needed to oversee and carry through the implementation plan • correct alchemy of pressure and support • early rewards for implementers • ongoing INSET to maintain commitment (*behaviours often change before beliefs*)
Institutionalisation	Innovation will be more successful if it: • becomes embedded into everyday practice • is clearly linked to classroom practice • is in widespread use across several classrooms, schools • is not contending with other priorities • is subject to continuing INSET for new staff

Figure 11.5   Fullan's model for successful change

Such a model operates at national, LEA and school level. At national level, for example, we can see that the political agenda is clear, a model has been provided via the KS3 Literacy conferences, a national figure to advocate change is in office (the Assistant Director of the National Literacy Strategy has been given responsibility for KS3 literacy) and the short timetable for the Year 7 intervention programme encourages early, active initiation. Readers may like to judge for themselves how far at national level we are into the implementation stage. Whether, nationally, we can see 'the correct alchemy of pressure and support' and 'early rewards for implementers' is a question which stimulates lively responses from secondary teachers!

In a useful timetable, showing a detailed planning cycle, Eve Bearne uses a modified version of Fullan's three stages – Year 1: Investigation, Year 2: Implementation, Year 3: Consolidation and Evaluation (Bearne 1999, pp. 264–6) which illustrates how Fullan's cycle can provide a framework for practical action at school level. Her three-year suggested timetable may now be too leisurely to be deemed wholly appropriate to the current situation and fails to fulfil the criteria of 'an early active initiation establishing initial commitment (*an elaborate planning stage is wasteful of energy*)'. Indeed, she recommends devoting a whole year to the planning stage. If this is compressed, however, the Bearne timetable contains much sensible advice.

We can see that the factors identified by Fullan generally coincide with those identified in school effectiveness research. Crucially, he identifies the importance of practices being perceived by teachers as something that will serve their and their pupils' needs. Put another way – if curriculum development is to be lasting, teachers need to make it their own and integrate it into their practice (Kennedy and Kennedy 1996).

Conclusion

If we map the factors identified from school effectiveness, school improvement and literacy research onto Fullan's cycle of implementation we can begin to see how schools might develop successful literacy initiatives. To schools' planned implementation and the development of a written policy we must add practical support from outside agencies via extra resources and a public acknowledgement of the importance of the task schools are being asked to undertake. The commitment of teachers will always be necessary to the success of new initiatives. Unless the present government, via LEAs where appropriate, can offer support to already busy teachers we may be in danger of another spate of short-term literacy initiatives with no lasting impact.

We have a renewed opportunity to make a difference to pupils' literacy in the secondary school. The language and literacy skills our pupils need to become citizens of the twenty-first century and the language and literacy teaching needed to achieve those skills will continue to be debated. That the goal, of improving literacy standards for all, is one worth striving for is, however, incontestable. All secondary teachers can play their part in achieving this goal. For our part we hope that through the work we have carried out, and stimulated, as part of the Nuffield EXEL project, a small part of which is reported in this book, we have played a role in enhancing literacy teaching and learning in our secondary schools.

Appendix 1

Contact list for Key Stage 3 literacy pilot projects

Based on information from School File for KS3 literacy conferences (DfEE 1999b)

LEA	Contact details
Barking and Dagenham	General Inspector – English Inspection and Advisory Service, Westbury Centre, Ripple Road, Barking JG11 7PT. Tel: 020 8270 4818 Fax: 020 8270 4811
Birmingham	Schools' Adviser – English Birmingham Advisory Service (BASS), Martineau Education Centre, Balden Road, Harborne, Birmingham B32 2EH. Tel: 0121 427 3020 Fax: 0121 4281196
Brighton and Hove	Schools' Adviser King's House, Grand Avenue, Hove BN3 2SU. Tel: 01273 293453 Fax: 01273 293599
Bristol	Divisional Director for Achievements The Bristol Centre, Sheridan Road, Horfield, Bristol BS7 OPU. Tel: 0117 931 1111 Fax: 0117 931 1619
Coventry	Language Adviser, Elm Bank Teachers' Centre, Coventry CV1 2LQ. Tel: 024 7652 7409 Fax: 024 7652 7468
Derbyshire	Senior Adviser Chatsworth Hall, Chesterfield Road, Matlock, Derbyshire DE4 3AC. Tel: 01629 580000 Ext. 5715 Fax: 01629 585466
Durham	English Inspector Education Department, County Hall, Durham DH1 5UJ. Tel: 0191 383 4556 Fax: 0191 383 4257
Ealing	General Inspector Perceval House, 14–16 Uxbridge Road, Ealing W5 2HL. Tel: 0181 5792424 Fax: 0181 8326198
Hertfordshire	KS3 Project Manager, Assessment Team Hertfordshire Services, The Education Centre, Butterfield Road, Wheathampstead, Herts AL4 8PY. Tel: 01582 830337 Fax: 01582 830335

(continued)

LEA	Contact details
Islington	KS3 Literacy Project Manager Barnsbury Centre, London N1 1TH. Tel: 020 7457 5657　　Fax: 020 7457 5500
Lambeth and Southwark	KS3 Literacy Project Director CLPE, Webber Street, London SE1 8QW. Tel: 020 7401 3382　　Fax: 020 7928 4624
Lancashire	English Adviser Advisory Division, Education Offices Buildings, Derby Street, Ormskirk L39 2BT. Tel: 0169 557 3971 Ext. 5755　　Fax: 0169 558 0305
Leicestershire	English Advisor County Hall, Glenfield, Leicester LE3 8RF. Tel: 0116 265 6446　　Fax: 0116 265 6550
Manchester	English Adviser Manchester Literacy Centre, Moston Campus, Ashley Lane, Manchester M9 4WU. Tel: 0161 205 1227　　Fax: 0161 205 1228
Newham	KS3 Strategy Manager INSEC, Kirton Road, London E13 9BT. Tel: 020 8548 5053　　Fax: 020 8471 4605
North Lincolnshire	Secondary Adviser – English Directorate of Education & Personnel Development, PO Box 35, Hewson House, Station Road, Brigg DN20 8XJ. Tel: 01724 297186　　Fax: 01724 297282
Nottingham City	Schools' Adviser Sandfield Centre, Lenton, Nottingham NG7 1QH. Tel: 0115 915 0628　　Fax: 0115 915 8040
Sheffield	Curriculum Adviser for English and Drama Education Department, Leopold Street, Sheffield, South Yorkshire S1 1RJ. Tel: 0114 2735672/2506847　　Fax: 0114 250648
Stockport	Senior Adviser Education Division, Stopford House, Stockport SK1 3XE. Tel: 0161 474 3923　　Fax: 0161 953 0085
West Sussex	English Adviser NEAPC, Furnace Drive, Crawley RH10 6JB. Tel: 01293553297　　Fax: 01293 533359
Wirral	General Inspector – English and Drama Wirral LEA, Hamilton Building, Conway Street, Birkenhead L41 4FD. Tel: 0151 666 4326　　Fax: 0151 666 4207

Key Objectives for Year 7, taken from The National Literacy Strategy Framework for Teaching

(From the LEA file, Key Stage 3 Literary Conferences, Summer Term 1999)

Word level work	Sentence level work	Text level work
Phonics, spelling and vocabulary	Grammar and punctuation	Comprehension and composition
Pupils should be taught:	*Pupils should be taught:*	*Pupils should be taught:*
Spelling strategies	**Grammatical awareness**	**Fiction and Poetry**
1. To secure spelling of words in List 3 (medial vowel phonemes).	1. To revise the language conventions and grammatical features of the different types of text such as:	*Reading and comprehension*
2. To identify misspelt words in own writing; to keep individual lists (e.g. spelling logs), to learn to spell them (*Y5 & 6*).	• narrative (e.g. stories and novels);	1. To articulate responses to literature, identifying why and how a text affects the reader.
3. To use known spellings as basis for spelling other words with similar patterns or related meanings (*Y5 & 6*).	• recounts (e.g. anecdotes, accounts of observations, experiences);	2. To investigate how characters are presented, referring to the text:
4. To use independent spelling strategies, including:	• instructional texts (e.g. instructions and directions);	• through dialogue, action and description;
• building up spellings by syllabic parts, using known prefixes, suffixes and common letter strings;	• reports (e.g. factual writing description);	• how the reader responds to them (as victims, heroes, etc.);
• applying knowledge of spelling rules and exceptions;	• explanatory texts (how and why);	• through examining their relationships with other characters (*Y5*).
	• persuasive texts (e.g. opinions, promotional literature);	3. To take account of viewpoint in a novel through:
	• discursive texts (e.g. balanced arguments) (*Y6*).	• identifying the narrator;
		• explaining how this influences the reader's view of events;

Word level (continued)	**Sentence level** (continued)	**Text level** (continued)
• building words from other known words, and from awareness of the meaning or derivations of words; • using dictionaries and IT spellchecks. • Using visual skills, e.g. recognising common letter strings and checking critical features (i.e. does it look right, shape, length, etc.) (*Y5*). 5. To practise new spellings regularly by 'look, say, cover, write, check' strategy (*Y4*). **Spelling conventions and rules** 1. To practise extending, and compounding words through adding parts, e.g. *ful, ly, ive, tion, ic, ist*; revise and reinforce earlier work on prefixes and suffixes; investigate links between meaning and spelling (*Y4*). 2. To investigate, collect and classify spelling patterns in pluralisation, construct rules for regular spellings, e.g. add *-s* to most words; add *-es* to most words ending in *-s, -sh, -ch*, change *-f* to *-ves*; when *-y* is preceded by a consonant, change to *-ies*; when *-y* is preceded by a vowel, add *-s* (*Y5*). 3. To explore spelling patterns of consonants and formulate rules: • *ll* in full becomes *l* when used as a suffix;	2. To discuss, proofread and edit their own writing for clarity and correctness, e.g. by creating more complex sentences, using a range of connectives, simplifying clumsy constructions (*Y5*). 3. To understand the difference between direct and reported speech (e.g. 'she said, "I am going"', 'she said she was going') through: • finding and comparing examples from reading; • discussing contexts and reasons for using particular forms and their effects; • transforming direct into reported speech and vice versa, noting changes in punctuation and words that have to be changed or added (*Y5*). 4. To revise and extend work on adjectives and link to work on expressive and figurative language in stories and poetry: • constructing adjectival phrases: • examining comparative and superlative adjectives; • comparing adjectives on a scale of intensity (e.g. hot, warm, tepid, lukewarm, chilly, cold); • relating them to the suffixes which indicate degrees of intensity (e.g. *-ish, -er, -est*); • relating them to adverbs which indicate degrees of	• explaining how events might look from a different point of view (*Y6*). 4. To understand how the use of expressive and descriptive language can, e.g. create moods, arouse expectations, build tension, describe attitude or emotion (*Y4*). 5. To understand how settings influence events and incidents in stories and affect characters' behaviour (*Y4*). 6. To understand the differences between literal and figurative language, e.g. through discussing the effects of imagery in poetry and prose. *Writing composition* 1. To manipulate narrative perspective by: • writing in voice and style of a text; • producing a modern retelling; • writing a story with two different narrators (*Y6*). 2. To plan quickly and effectively the plot, characters and structure of their own narrative writing (*Y6*). 3. To write discursively about a novel or story, e.g. to explain or comment on it (*Y5*).

Word level (continued)	Sentence level (continued)	Text level (continued)
• words ending with a single consonant preceded by a short vowel double the consonant before adding -*ing*, etc. e.g. *hummed, sitting, wetter*; • *c* is usually soft when followed by *i*, e.g. *circus, accident* (Y5). 4. To spell unstressed vowels in polysyllabic words, e.g. *company, portable, poisonous, interest, description, carpet, sector, freedom, extra*. 5. To investigate and learn spelling rules: • words ending in modifying *e*, drop *e* when adding *ing*, e.g. *taking*; • words ending in modifying *e*, keep *e* when adding a suffix beginning with a consonant, e.g. *hopeful lovely*; • words ending in *y* preceded by a consonant, change *y* to *ie* when adding a suffix, e.g. *flies, tried* – except for the suffixes *ly* or *ing*, e.g. *shyly, flying*; • *i* before *e* except after *c* when the sound is *ee*, e.g. *receive*. Note and learn the exceptions 6. To transform words, e.g. • changing tenses: *ed, -ing*; • negation: *un, im, il*; • making comparatives: *er, est, ish*; • changing verbs to nouns: *ion, ism, ology*; • nouns to verbs: *ise, ify, en* (Y5).	intensity (e.g. very, quite, more, most) and through investigating words which can be intensified in these ways and words which cannot (Y4). **Sentence construction and punctuation** 1. From reading, to understand how dialogue is set out, e.g. on separate lines for alternate speakers in narrative, and the positioning of commas before speech marks (Y5). 2. To investigate connecting words and phrases: • collect examples from reading and thesauruses; • study how points are typically connected in different kinds of text; • classify useful examples for different kinds of text, e.g. by position (*besides, nearby, by*); sequence (*firstly, secondly, …*); logic (*so, therefore, consequently*); • identify connectives which have multiple purposes (e.g. *on, under, besides*) (Y6). 3. To form complex sentences through, e.g.: • using different connecting devices; • reading back complex sentences for clarity of meaning, and adjusting as necessary; • evaluating which links work best; • exploring how meaning is affected by the sequence	**Non-fiction** *Reading comprehension* 1. To review a range of non-fiction text types and their characteristics, discussing when a writer might choose to write in a given style and form (Y6). 2. To secure understanding of the features of non-chronological reports: • introductions to orientate reader; • use of generalisations to categorise; • language to describe; and, • differentiate; • impersonal language; • mostly present tense (Y6). 3. To identify how and why paragraphs are used to organise and sequence information (Y4). 4. To identify the key features of impersonal formal language, e.g. the present tense, the passive voice and discuss when and why they are used (Y6). 5. Note-making: to fillet passages for relevant information and present ideas which are effectively grouped and linked (Y5). *Writing composition* 1. To plan, compose, edit and refine short non-chronological reports and explanatory texts, using reading as a source, focusing on clarity, conciseness, and impersonal style (Y5).

Word level (continued)	Sentence level (continued)	Text level (continued)
7. To revise and consolidate work from previous terms with particular emphasis on: • learning and inventing spelling rules; • inventing and using mnemonics for irregular or difficult spelling. **Vocabulary extension** 1. To use alternative words and expressions which are more accurate or interesting than the common choices, e.g. *got, nice, good, then, said* (*Y4*). 2. To build a bank of useful terms and phrases for argument, e.g. *similarly . . . whereas . . .* (*Y6*).	and structure of clauses (*Y6*). 4. To recognise how commas, connectives and full stops are used to join and separate clauses; to identify in their writing where each is more effective (*Y4*). 5. To use punctuation effectively to signpost meaning in longer and more complex sentences (*Y5*).	2. To divide whole texts into paragraphs, paying attention to the sequence of paragraphs and to the links between one paragraph and the next, e.g. through the choice of appropriate connectives (*Y6*). 3. To select the appropriate style and form to suit a specific purpose and audience, drawing on knowledge of different non-fiction text types.

References

Action Aid (1992) *Nairobi: Kenyan City Life*. Frome: Action Aid.

Adult Literacy and Basic Skills Unit (ALBSU) (1995) *Older and younger: the basic skills of different age groups*. London: ALBSU.

Alessi, S., Anderson, T. and Goetz, E. (1979) 'An investigation of lookbacks during studying', *Discourse Processes* **2**, 197–212.

Anderson, T. (1980) 'Study strategies and adjunct aids', in Spiro, R., Bruce, B. and Brewer, W. (eds) *Theoretical Issues in Reading Comprehension*. Hillsdale, New Jersey: Lawrence Erlbaum.

Baker, L. and Brown, A. (1984) 'Metacognitive skills and reading', in Pearson, D. (ed.) *Handbook of Reading Research*. New York: Longman.

Bandura, A. (1992) '*Perceived self-efficacy in cognitive development and functioning*'. Address given at the annual meeting of the American Education Research Association, San Francisco, April 1992.

Beard, R. (1987) *Developing Reading 3–13*. London: Hodder & Stoughton.

Beard, R. (1993) *Teaching Literacy Balancing Perspectives*. London: Hodder & Stoughton.

Bearne, E. (1999) *Use of Language Across the Secondary Curriculum*. London: Routledge.

Bennetts, T. (1995) 'Continuity and progression', *Teaching Geography* **20**(2), 75–80.

Bereiter, C. and Scardamalia, M. (1987) *The psychology of written composition*. Hillsdale, New Jersey: Lawrence Erlbaum Associates.

Bereiter, C. and Scardamalia, M. (1993) 'Composing and writing', in Beard, R. (ed.) *Teaching Literacy Balancing Perspectives*. London: Hodder & Stoughton.

Brookover, W. *et al.* (1979) *School social systems and students' achievement: schools can make a difference*. New York: Praeger.

Brooks, G., Pugh, A. and Schagen, I. (1996) *Reading performance at nine*. Slough: National Foundation for Educational Research.

Brookes, W. and Goodwyn, A. (1998) 'Literacy in the secondary school'. Paper given at the 1998 British Educational Research Association conference, Queens University.

Brown, A. (1979) 'Theory of memory and the problems of development: activity, growth and knowledge', in Cermak, L. and Craik, F. (eds) *Levels of Processing in Human Memory*. Hillsdale, New Jersey: Lawrence Erlbaum.

Brown, A. (1980) 'Metacognitive development and reading', in Spiro, R., Bruce, B. and Brewer, W. (eds) *Theoretical Issues in Reading Comprehension*. Hillsdale, New Jersey: Lawrence Erlbaum.

Cairney, T. (1990) *Teaching Reading Comprehension*. Milton Keynes: Open University Press.

Catron, J. (1997) 'Literacy: a policy for everyone', *The Secondary English Magazine* **1**(1), 9–11.

Caul, L. (1994) 'School effectiveness in Northern Ireland: illustration and practice'. Paper for the Standing Commission on Human Rights.

Chambers, A. (1993) *Tell Me: Children, Reading and Talk*. Stroud: Thimble Press.

Child, D. (1973) *Psychology and the Teacher*. London: Holt, Rinehart & Winston.

Christie, F. (1985) *Language Education*. Oxford: Oxford University Press.

Cohen, M. (1983) 'Instructional, management and social conditions in effective schools', in Webb, A. O. and Webb, L. D. (eds) *School finance and school improvement: linkages in the 1980s*. Cambridge, Mass.: Ballinger.

Collins, J. and Dallat, J. (1998) 'Reading at Key Stage 3: A Northern Ireland survey of provision and need', *Journal of In-Service Education* **24**(3), 467 –74.

Cooper, H. *et al.* (1996). 'The effects of summer vacation on achievement test scores: a narrative and meta-analytical review', *Review of Educational Research* **66**(3), 227–68.

Counsell, C. (1997) *Analytical and Discursive Writing at Key Stage 3*. Shaftesbury: The Historical Association.

Creemers, B. P. M. (1994) 'The history, value and purpose of school effectiveness studies', in Reynolds, D. (ed.) *Advances in school effectiveness research and practice*. Oxford: Pergamon.

Cudd, E. T. (1989) 'Research and Report Writing in the Elementary Grades', *The Reading Teacher* **43**(4), 268–9.

Czerniewska, P. (1992) *Learning about Writing*. Oxford: Blackwell.

de Castell, S. and Luke, A. (1986) 'Models of literacy in North American schools: social and historical conditions and consequences', in de Castell, S., Luke, A. and Egan, K. (eds) *Literacy, Society and Schooling*. Cambridge: Cambridge University Press.

Department of Education and Science (DES) (1975) *A Language for Life*. (The Bullock Report). London: HMSO.

Department for Education and Employment (DfEE) (1997a) *The Implementation of the National Literacy Strategy*. London: HMSO.

Department for Education and Employment (DfEE) (1997b) *Secondary Literacy: a survey by HMI Autumn Term 1997*. DfEE.

Department for Education and Employment (DfEE) (1997c) *Excellence in Schools*. DfEE.

Department for Education and Employment (DfEE) (1998a) *Review of Secondary Education 1993–97*. DfEE.

Department for Education and Employment (DfEE) (1998b) Letter to LEAs who were successful in their bid for KS3 literacy funding. London: DfEE.

Department for Education and Employment (DfEE) (1998c) *The National Literacy Strategy framework of objectives*. London: HMSO.

Department for Education and Employment (DfEE) (1999a) *Radical change needed to boost basic skills. A briefing paper on the report 'A Fresh Start – Improving Literacy and Numeracy'*. Skills and Enterprise Briefing, Issue 5/99.

Department for Education and Employment (DfEE) (1999b) *The National Literacy Strategy Key Stage 3 Literacy Conferences*. LEA File, School File and video. London: DfEE.

Department for Education and Employment (DfEE) (1999c) *National Literacy Strategy Guidance for providers of Summer Literacy Schools and Key Stage 3 Intervention programmes for literacy in 1999–2000.* London: DfEE (reference code SLSKS3).

Development Education Association (1996) *Global Perspectives in the National Curriculum: Guidance for Key Stage 3 Geography.* Development Education Association.

Development Education Centre (Birmingham) (1995) *Development Compass Rose – a consultation pack.*

Dew-Hughes, D., Brayton, H. and Blandford, S. (1998) A survey of training and professional development for learning support assistants, *Support for Learning* **13**(4), 179–83.

Ebbinghaus, H. (1966) *Memory.* New York: Dover.

Ekinsmyth, C. and Bynner, J. (1994) *The Basic Skills of Young Adults.* London: ALBSU.

EXEL (1995) *Writing Frames.* Exeter University School of Education. (This booklet is now published as Lewis, M. and Wray, D. (1997) *Writing Frames*, Reading and Language Information Centre, University of Reading.)

Frater, G. (1997) *Improving Boys' Literacy.* London: Basic Skills Agency.

Fullan, M. (1988) 'Managing curriculum change', in *The dynamics of curriculum change: curriculum at the crossroads.* London: School Curriculum Development Committee.

Fullan, M. (1991) *The new meaning of educational change.* London: Cassell.

Galton, M. (1987) 'Change and continuity in the Primary School: the research evidence', *Oxford Review of Education* **13**(1), 81–93.

Garner, R. (1987) *Metacognition and Reading Comprehension.* Norwod, New Jersey: Ablex.

Goodman, K. (1985) 'Unity in reading', in Singer, H. and Ruddell, R. (eds) *Theoretical Models and Processes of Reading.* Newark, Delaware: International Reading Association.

Goringe, P. and Mason, S. (1995) The Quality of Learning in Years 6 and 7. Oxford: National Primary Centre.

Graves, M. F. and Graves, B. B. (1995) 'The scaffolded reading experience: a flexible framework for helping children get the most out of text', *Reading* **29**(1), 29–34.

Gray, J. (1990) 'The quality of schooling: framework for judgements', *British Journal of Educational Studies* **38**(3), 204–33.

Hanley, S. (1994) *On Constructivism.* Maryland Collaborative for Teacher Preparation, The University of Maryland. Available at http://www.inform.umd.edu/UMS+State/UMDProjects/MCTP/Essays/Constructivism.txt

Harrison, C. and Salinger, T. (1998) *Assessing Reading 1: Theory and Practice.* London: Routledge.

Harrison, C., Bailey, M. and Dewar, A. (1998) 'Responsive reading assessment: is postmodern assessment of reading possible?' in Harrison, C. and Salinger, T. (eds) *Assessing Reading 1: Theory and Practice.* London: Routledge.

Hayward, L. and Spencer, E. (1998) 'Taking a closer look: a Scottish perspective on reading assessment' in Harrison, C. and Salinger, T. (eds) *Assessing Reading 1: Theory and Practice.* London: Routledge.

Hertrich, J. (1999a) 10 critical dimensions arising from the Key Stage 3 projects, www.literacytrust.org.uk

Hertrich, J. (1999b) 18 issues deriving from HMI's inspection of the projects, www.literacytrust.org.uk

Higgins, G. (1995) 'Work with parents in a secondary school in Glasgow', *Literacy Today* **2**, 16–17.

Huggins, M. and Knight, P. (1997) 'Curriculum continuity and transfer from Primary to Secondary school: the case of history', *Educational Studies* **23**(3), 333–48.

Jones, B., Swift, D. and Vickers, D. 'Writing about development', *Teaching Geography* **22**(1), 5–10.

Kennedy, C. and Kennedy, J. (1996) 'Teachers' attitudes to change implementation', *System* **24**(3), 351–60.

Language and Curriculum access Service (LcaS) (1997) *Making progress in Humanities: scaffolding learning in the multilingual classrooms.* London Borough of Enfield.

Leat, D. (1997) 'Cognitive Acceleration in Geographical Education', in Tilbury, D. and Williams, M. (eds) *Teaching and Learning in Geography.* London: Routledge.

Leat, D. (1998) *Thinking Through Geography.* Cambridge: Chris Kington Publishing.

Lee, B., Harris, S. and Dickson, P. (1995) *Continuity and Progression 5–16: Developments in Schools.* Slough: NFER.

Lewis, M. and Wray, D. (1999) 'Secondary teachers' views about literacy and literacy teaching', *Educational Review* **51**(3), 273–81.

Lewis, M., Wray, D. and Rospigliosi, P. (1995) 'No copying please! Helping children respond to non-fiction text', *Education 3–13*, **23**(1), 27–34.

Lezotte, L. (1989) 'School improvement based on the effective schools research', *International Journal of Educational Research* **13**(7), 815–25.

Literacy Task Force (1997) *A reading revolution: How we can teach every child to read well.* London: Literacy Task Force.

Littlefair, A. (1991) *Reading All Types of Writing.* Milton Keynes: Open University Press.

Lunzer, E. and Gardner, K. (1979) *The Effective Use of Reading.* Oxford: Heinemann.

Lunzer, E. and Gardner, K. (1984) *Learning from the written word.* Edinburgh: Oliver & Boyd.

Marland, M. (ed.) (1981) *Information Skills in the Secondary Curriculum.* London: Methuen.

Martin, J. (1985) *Factual Writing: Exploring and Challenging Social Reality.* Oxford: Oxford University Press.

Medwell, J. *et al.* (1998) *Effective teachers of literacy.* A report commissioned by the Teacher Training Agency. London: TTA.

Meek, M. (1988) *How Texts Teach What Readers Learn.* Bath: Thimble Press.

Mercer, N. (1995) *The Guided Construction of Knowledge.* Clevedon: Multilingual Matters.

Merritt, J. E. (1979) 'The importance of valid assessment', in Raggett, M., Tutt, C. and Raggett, P. (eds) *Assessment and Testing of Reading: Problems and Practices.* London: Ward Lock Educational.

Morgan, R. (1986) *Helping children read.* London: Methuen.

Mortimore, P. (1993) 'School effectiveness and the management of effective teaching and learning', *School effectiveness and school improvement* **4**(4), 290–310.

Mortimore, P. (1994) 'The positive effects of schooling', in Rutter, M. (ed) *Youth in the Year 2000: phycho–social issues and interventions.* Boston: Cambridge University Press.

Mortimore, P. *et al.* (1988) *School Matters: The Junior Years.* Wells: Open Books.

Neate, B. (1992) *Finding Out about Finding Out.* London: Hodder & Stoughton.

North-West Regional Education Laboratory (NREL) (1990) *Onward to excellence: effective schooling Practices: a research synthesis.* Portland, Oregon: NREL.

Nutbrown, C. (1999) 'Purpose and authenticity in early literacy assessment', *Reading* **33**(1), 33–40.

Office for Standards in Education (OFSTED) (1999) *The National Literacy Strategy. An Interim Evaluation.*

Ogle, D. M. (1986) 'A teaching model that develops active reading of expository text', *The Reading Teacher* **39**(6).

Ogle, D. M. (1989) 'The Know, Want to Know, Learn Strategy', in Muth, K. D. (ed.) *Children's Comprehension of Text.* Newark, Delaware: International Reading Association.

Open University E825 (1994) *Study Guide: Language and Literacy in Social Context.* Milton Keynes: The Open University.

Palincsar, A. and Brown, A. (1984) 'Reciprocal teaching of comprehension-fostering and comprehension-monitoring activities', *Cognition and Instruction* **1**(2), 117–75.

Pearson, P., Destefane, L. and Garcia, G. (1998) 'Ten dilemmas of performance assessment', in Harrison, C. and Salinger, T. (eds) *Assessing Reading 1: Theory and Practice.* London: Routledge.

Plackett, E. (1999) 'Review of "Use of language across the secondary Curriculum"', *English and Media Magazine* **40**.

Purkey, S. C. and Smith, M. S. (1983) 'Effective schools: a review', *Elementary Schools Journal* **83**(4), 427–52.

Qualifications and Curriculum Authority (QCA) (1998) *Building Bridges: Guidance and Training Materials for Teachers of Year 6 and Year 7 Pupils.* London: QCA.

Qualifications and Curriculum Authority (QCA) (1999) *Consultation documents on the review of the national curriculum*, www.qca.org.uk

Raggett, M., Tutt, C. and Raggett, P. (eds) *Assessment and Testing of Reading: Problems and Practices.* London: Ward Lock Educational.

Reynolds, D. (1998) 'Schooling for literacy: a review of research on teacher effectiveness and its implications for contemporary educational policies', *Educational Review* **50**(20) 147–61.

Robinson, S. and Hertrich, J. (1998) *Key Stage 3 Literacy: A survey by HMI, Autumn Term, 1998,* www.literacytrust.org.uk

Rumelhart, D. (1980) 'Schemata: the building blocks of cognition', in Spiro, R., Bruce, B. and Brewer, W. (eds) *Theoretical Issues in Reading Comprehension.* Hillsdale, New Jersey: Lawrence Erlbaum.

Rumelhart, D. (1985) 'Toward an interactive model of reading', in Singer, H. and Ruddell, R. (eds) *Theoretical Models and Processes of Reading.* Newark, Delaware: International Reading Association.

Rutter, M. *et al.* (1979) *Fifteen Thousand Hours: Secondary Schools and Their Effect on Children.* London: Open Books.

Sainsbury, M. *et al.* (1998) 'Fallback in attainment on Transfer at age 11: evidence from the Summer Literacy Schools evaluation', *Educational Research Journal* **40**(1), 73–81.

Sammons, P., Hillman, J. and Mortimore, P. (1995) *Key Characteristics of Effective Schools: A Review of School Effectiveness Research.* (A report by the London Institute of Education for the Office for Standards in Education). London: Institute of Education.

Schagen, S. and Kerr, D. (1999) *Bridging the Gap? The National Curriculum and Progression from Primary to Secondary School.* Slough: NFER.

Scheerens, J. (1992) *Effective Schooling: research, theory and practice.* London: Cassell.

School Curriculum and Assessment Authority (SCAA) (1997) *Use of Language: A Common Approach.* London: SCAA.

Sheeran, Y. and Barnes, D. (1991) *School Writing: Discovering the Ground Rules*. Buckingham: Open University Press.

Slavin, R. E. (1987) 'Co-operative learning and the co-operative school', *Educational Leadership* **45**, 7–13.

Stierer, B. (1994) '"Simply doing their job?" The politics of reading standards and "real books"', in Stierer, B. and Maybin, J. (eds) *Language, Learning and Literacy in Educational Practice*. Clevedon: Multilingual Matters.

Tizard, J., Schofield, W. N. and Hewison, J. (1982) 'Collaboration between teachers and parents in assisting children's reading', *British Journal of Educational Psychology* **52**, 1–15.

Tizard, B. *et al.* (1988) *Young Children at School in the Inner City*. Hove: Laurence Erlbaum.

Tonjes, M. (1988) 'Metacognitive modelling and glossing: two powerful ways to teach self responsibility', in Anderson, C. (ed.) *Reading: The ABC and Beyond*. Basingstoke: Macmillan.

Topping, K. and Wolfendale, S. (eds) (1985) *Parental Involvement in Children's Reading*. London: Croom Helm.

United Nations Education, Scientific and Cultural Organisation (UNESCO) (1999) *Statistical Database: Illiteracy, UK 1997*. www.unescostat.unesco.org

United States Department of Education (1987) *What works? Research about teaching and learning*. Washington: Department of Education.

Vygotsky L. (1962/1978) *Thought and Language*. Cambridge, Mass.: MIT. (1978 is titled *Mind in Society: The Development of Higher Psychological Processes*, Harvard University Press. (Later edition, 1986.)).

Webster, A., Beveridge, M. and Reed, M. (1996) *Managing the Literacy Curriculum*. London: Routledge.

Weindling, D. (1989) 'The process of school improvement: some practical messages from research', *School Organisation* **9**(1).

Wells, G. (1987) *The Meaning Makers: Children Learning Language and Using Language to Learn*. London: Hodder and Stoughton Educational.

Winchester, S. (1995) *Individualised Assessment of Children's Reading Development*. Birmingham: Birmingham LEA Assessment Unit.

Winkworth, E. (1977) *User Education in Schools*. Boston: British Library Research and Development Department.

Wittgenstein, L. (1922) *Tractatus Logico-Philosophicus* (translated by C. K. Ogden). London: Routledge Kegan Paul.

Wragg, E. C. *et al.* (1998) *Improving Literacy in the Primary School*. London: Routledge.

Wray, D. (1981) *Extending Reading Skills*. Lancaster: University of Lancaster.

Wray, D. (1985) *Teaching Information Skills through Project Work*. London: Hodder & Stoughton.

Wray, D. (1988) 'Literacy: the information dimension', in Anderson, C. (ed.) *Reading: the ABC and Beyond*. London: Macmillan Education.

Wray, D. (1994) *Literacy and Awareness*. London: Hodder & Stoughton.

Wray, D. and Lewis, M. (1992) 'Primary pupils' use of information books', *Reading* **26**(3), 19–24.

Wray, D. and Lewis, M. (1997) *Extending Literacy: Children Reading and Writing Non-fiction*. London: Routledge.

Wray, D. and Medwell, J. (1991) *Literacy and Language in the Primary Years*. London: Routledge.

Wray, D. and Rogers, S. (1997) *Lewisham Literacy 2000: An interim evaluation*. Lewisham: London Borough of Lewisham Education Authority.

Index